UNSTOPPABLE!

Just when everyone was wondering what the folks at Nintendo were gonna do for an encore, the Game Boy system made its electrifying debut! Game Boy is a system that does away with bulky hardware and that listless "always in front of the living-room TV" feeling. Now you can take the thrill of Nintendo® games with you anywhere, be it the local swimming pool, on vacation, or while buying groceries—though we don't advise your using it in class the day of the big exam!

And just when you were undoubtedly wondering what videogame legend Jeff Rovin was going to do as a follow-up to his titanic bestsellers *How to Win at Nintendo Games 1, 2, 3, Sports* and *Super Mario Bros.*, here comes ol' Jeff again, with just the Game Boy system guidebook you've been looking for.

Packed with facts, tactics, and overall strategies for coming out on top of the best and most exciting games you can play on the Game Boy system—and let's not forget Jeff's special added attraction of tips on winning at Atari's Lynx system—*How to Win at Game Boy Games* is the *only* unofficial guide you'll ever need to understanding what makes the Game Boy and Lynx systems tick!

HOW TO WIN AT GAME BOY GAMES

With a special section
of tips on winning at
Atari's Lynx System!

JEFF ROVIN

ST. MARTIN'S PAPERBACKS

How to Win at Game Boy Games is an unofficial guide, not endorsed by Nintendo® or Atari®.

Nintendo is a registered trademark and Game Boy is a trademark of Nintendo of America, Inc. Atari is a registered trademark and Lynx is a trademark of Atari Corporation.

HOW TO WIN AT GAME BOY GAMES

ISBN: 0-312-92632-4

Printed in the United States of America

St. Martin's Paperbacks edition/June 1991

10 9 8 7 6 5 4 3 2

CONTENTS

CONTENTS

INTRODUCTION

Who'd have thought it?

Who'd have believed that in an age of vibrant color games and increasingly bigger TV screens, a small, black and white screen could captivate videogame players?

Well, it's happened.

In less than two years Game Boy has become one of the most popular toys in the United States, the release of each new cartridge awaited as eagerly as the arrival of every new Nintendo Entertainment System game.

The reason for its popularity is simple. In addition to portability, Game Boy features wonderfully fluid graphics and terrific sound, a diverse selection of games, and the same spine-tingling, white-knuckle, toe-curling thrills as NES games.

And, of course, it presents a slew of new challenges that cry out for a handy book of tips!

Like our series of books on winning at Nintendo Games, *How to Win at Game Boy Games* is a step-by-step guide to beating the best and most popular of the Game Boy cartridges. The book is also a handy guide to what's good and bad in every Game

Boy cartridge—things you'll want to know before buying a particular game.

Each game is broken down as follows:

Type: In a nutshell, what the game is.

Object: A detailed look at the story of the game.

Hero: What powers and abilities do you have while you play?

Villains: What kinds of enemies and obstacles do you face?

Points: How you get them, and whether or not there's a timer.

Strategy: Detailed tips on how to win. For a number of games, such as *Batman* and *The Castlevania Adventure*, you'll notice that we've given extensive coverage to the early levels, while providing only vital tips for the last level. The reason for this is simple: once you get the hang of playing, a blow-by-blow description of later levels is redundant and space-consuming. If you've gotten to level four in *The Castlevania Adventure* and aren't sure how to beat a Zeldo, describing it again isn't going to help!

Rating: Would you be better off spending your money elsewhere? We'll give you the lowdown.

As ever, we welcome your comments; simply write in care of the publisher. A favor, though: if you want a response, please include a postcard or a self-addressed, *stamped* envelope. Otherwise, we won't have enough money left for Game Boy games!

See you in the next book, and—happy videogaming!

BAD 'N RAD

Type: Skateboarding with obstacles

Object: The town of Vileville has been rocked by the evil ElRad's abduction of the beloved Miss Ariel. As Ariel's boyfriend, and a top skateboarder, you must brave ElRad's defenses to rescue her.

Hero: While riding your Skateboard, you can duck under low-hanging objects or leap over things on the ground. You can also pound enemies by landing on them. Big Dip, Pizza, and Canned Goodies add life points when you run across them; there are other power-ups as well.

Villains: These are discussed in the instruction booklet. The clock is also your foe, as you have a limited amount of time to complete each stage.

Points: You earn points for gathering goodies, landing on your enemies, and defeating Bosses. Win enough points, and you'll be rewarded with a one-up.

Strategy: Skateboarding through each stage you'll find the following:

Stage One: The view in this stage is from the side as you go through the city streets. You can Board right through to the first Ramp without stopping: just jump the two Tires rolling at you—or jump up *into* them with the front of your Skateboard and destroy them for points—keep going and the Flower Pot will fall behind you, then Board down the Ramp. On the other side you'll hop to a series of Walls to collect power-ups, then back down to the street; you should be able to do all of this without stopping. Once you come down, don't stop, and once again the Flower Pots will miss you. After the Pots fall, duck and Board under the Spikes. Stay crouched on the other side until after you've passed another bunch of Pots, get up on the Wall and collect the power-ups while avoiding the Deputy Dog. As soon as you come down, a second Dog will attack, so be prepared to bop it. You're free of danger through the second Ramp. On the way down, a hefty leap will earn you a one-up. Reaching the other side, you'll have to duck under more Spikes, leap onto a narrow Ledge, then lift your Skateboard up and land on top of Sir Slice Alot. Jump another Pit after him, but beware: the Ledge you land on will collapse after just a few seconds. A series of Pits will follow: make sure you drop down onto the last part of the Street from the final section of Wall; otherwise, you'll plummet into a pit at the end—and miss the Big Dip there to boot! After beating a second Sir Slice Alot by bopping him with your board, you'll find yourself in an enormous playroom. Duck the second Ball from the right—the first won't hit you, and the remainder must be jumped (not just when they come at you the first time, but when they bounce)—and be prepared to battle the Clown. He'll throw Balls at you: use the bottom of your Skateboard to send them back at him.

Stage Two: This one's an overhead view as you race along a road beside the Beach; there are Ramps to the right and left of the road. Now—you can stay on the road until after the Fish Hook or you can reap slightly more power-ups by going at once to the water's edge and getting the Soda Cans there, then cutting back to the road. Experienced players will make their own way, so this is for beginners. Staying on the road and keeping up a quick pace (controller pressed to the bottom), leap the two Walls, collect the Can, then jump the second of the two Drums. Get the next two Cans, hop the Drum, jump the Wall, leap the first and third Drum, then cut to the right after you pass the Spikes. *Stay on the right,* even though it looks like you'll get nabbed by the Fish Hook: you won't. It'll move to the left. After passing under the Bridge, cut to the far left to avoid the Spikes coming up in the center. You can ride the Ramp to the left to get around them: if you hit it with enough speed, you'll go up and around the Spikes. But that's a tricky maneuver, so beginners will want to stay to the left of the Arrows on the road and jump the narrow section of Spikes looming ahead. (When you get really good, you can also leap the Spikes over the center!) Cut right toward the beach, quickly, so that you're on the sands when the two Drums come rolling from the left: you can't jump the Drums while you're on the Ramp! When the Drums are gone, collect the wealth of power-ups on the beach, including Pizza; remain on the sand, on the far right side, until you pass the Spikes up ahead—you don't have to jump these; there's a path on the right. Make sure that when you go through here you're going pretty quickly, so you'll have enough oomph to get back up to the road. Cut back up to the road in a hurry, since a Drum will come rolling at you from the left—easily avoided if you get up there fast enough. (If the Drum *does* hit you, don't try to get back up to the left: you won't make it. Instead, head to the far right and squeeze through the lane between the Spikes and the water.) After this are Spikes on your right, then three Drums. Stay to the left until you're past another set of Spikes on the right, cutting to the right *immediately* after you ride around them on the Ramp—or jump their thin left-hand side. If you don't head right, you'll be hit by the Drum that comes from the left; heading right gives you a chance to touch down and hop up again before it arrives. You'll come to another Bridge with a Fish Hook; again, stay to the right as you pass under. More Spikes follow, after which stay on the road: there are Spikes on both sides, and you can only survive if you're in the center. There's a thin row of Spikes, easily avoided, up ahead, followed by a huge row of death: cut up to the left Ramp as close as you can to these Spikes, since you'll need to stay up there awhile to pass them! Stay in the center of the road until you're past the Spikes that line both Ramps, then shift to the left: you've no choice now but to jump, and the goin's better on that side. Leaping this will bring you to stage three. (Nope . . . there's no Boss to fight. You must've scared 'im away by whipping the Clown!)

Stage Three: Another side-view screen this time around. The key to making it through this level is to jump at the very edge of every Pit: do that, and you'll make it across just about any obstacle. As you begin, you'll notice Rats leaving the sewer Drains on the wall—one from the second, two from the third, and one from the fourth. After that you'll come to a collapsing Bridge with a Rat in the middle. If it hits you, you're dead: the Bridge'll fall apart by the time you recover. Just attack the Bridge running and don't stop. Getting to the Ledges beyond, take a high jump at the very end of the cliff to the second Ledge and clobber the leaping Fish on your way down. Landing on the flippered fiend will carry you to the end of the Ledges. A Bridge and Two Rats combination follows, after which you've got to duck a set of Spikes, leap Pits with Dragons in 'em—the serpents from the package art—duck another set of Spikes, leap to a collapsing Ledge—hit it in the middle for the best "kick" over the Pit, and get off it *instantly*—then hop over a series of Harpoons being thrust from the bottom of the screen (four in all), attacks that alternate with more Spikes (also four).

When you're through with this section, you'll jump from Ledge to Ledge where there's a rising and falling water level. Obviously, if you're on a Ledge that gets submerged, you'll be slowed to a crawl . . . like the kind you do in a pool! This section is made "interesting" by sewer Drains that spew water at you. You don't want to get hit by the gushing water or miss a Ledge, so either jump over the Drains as you Board along or slow down and wait on the Ledge until the water stops. (If you do the latter, you'll have to backtrack a bit before continuing. Otherwise, you won't have enough speed to make the jump. Just don't take too long backtracking or you're liable to leap just when the next flood comes pouring from the Drain!)

After you pass the Drains, take high jumps from the very edge of each successive Ledge to avoid the Mines in the four Pits between 'em. Sonic Boomer is waiting for you beyond (land on his head), with two more Snakes in the Pit after him. The thing about these Snakes, though, is that you've got to hop from the head of one to the head of another in order to get across the Pit. That done, you've got more Ledges to cross . . . but not by jumping, since there are low Spikes overhead. Instead, press B and left on the pad and you'll simply Board right across . . . though you have to leap from the last one to get back to shore. More mines follow. After beating another Sonic Boomer, it's time to fight Mister Wart Monger, who'll rise from the water, attack you, descend, and rise again. Making life even more difficult are pesky Fish. All you have to do is peer into the murky depths, watching the Monger's moves . . . and go where he isn't. When he surfaces, leap on him as you did the Clown.

Stage Four: Back to the overhead view, and you'll be riding the Ramps a *lot* more than before! When you do, don't come down too early: the Pipes have Spikes on the sides, and if you come down too soon, you'll be impaled. The four Walls and five Rats that start this stage are easy. Shift slightly to the right after the third Can so you can scoop up the last Can and Pizza without much effort. After the fifth Rat, stay in the center of the road so you'll pass between the Pipes up ahead, then leap the Pool, cut to the right, swing right again, then return to the center to pass between the next two Pipes. Stay on the right for three full swings, return to the center to pass between the Pipes there, ride to the right, then get back to the center *carefully:* there are Spikes on the inside of these Pipes too! The good news is that there's a one-up here. Immediately afterward you'll start riding the Ramps almost constantly to get around the Grates—it's easier than jumping them; do so by alternating right and left sides. In any case, you'll have no choice but to *keep moving,* since a giant Roller shows up after a while to press you flat if you slow down. Just watch out for the Rat Holes while you're riding these last Ramps: they'll kill you!

Stage Five: In this overhead view round, stay to the right of center in order to negotiate the turns. Avoid the Eagle that attacks from the top and then the bottom, then leap the Spikes that stick from the sides. Watch out for weak sections of roadway: jump anything that doesn't look like it'll hold your weight. (The reason? It won't!) Upon reaching the Spiked Tunnels, stay smack in the middle: though the Walls move toward you, you'll be safe there. When you emerge, a Chopper will descend. Avoid it until you reach the next Tunnel, and it'll total itself on the cliff face as you enter. Clearing this phase, you'll have to negotiate a Tightrope: take it with a sideward stance, as though you were cutting a corner.

Stage Six: The last stage offers a side view. Crackling flames shoot from the top and bottom of the Cave: edge past them, then defeat the Sonic Boomer as before. On the Slopes, leap the Pits—but, obviously, not so high that you hit the Spikes above, and not so fast that you career into the Spikes up ahead (there's just enough room for you to duck under them). More rising and falling Ledges await: you can try to take them in a succession of leaps from the very edge, or take them one at a time, backing up a bit on each before vaulting to the next. Take out the Sonic Boomer ahead, then keep an eye on the Spikes overhead: one will drop down and turn itself into a humanoid enemy. Stay to the right and don't be daunted: a bop on the noggin with the Skateboard will take him out. Enter the doorway beyond and get set for the nastiest Slopes yet, with more Spikes than ever. Get through here and you'll come face to face with the supreme boss. The essence of beating him is to leap him when you can, hitting him as you do so. To avoid his Knives, stay on the very edge of the upper sections of floor after you've jumped him.

Rating: B+

You'll have a grand time with this game, though once in a while you'll wish you could return to life exactly where you died. Repeating the same sections over and over can get dreary! But that's a minor quarrel with an otherwise super cartridge!

BALLOON KID

Type: *Joust* type flying game

Object: Little Alice and Jim love playing with Balloons. One day, however, Jim is holding a batch of Balloons and is swept into the air by a strong wind. Taking to the air herself, Alice sets out after him, tracking him by collecting the Balloons he's left behind while avoiding various obstacles.

Hero: You can alter Alice's altitude and send her flying back and forth. On the ground, Alice can walk on any solid surface, including the backs of enemies. In addition to gathering regular Balloons, Alice can collect power-up Balloons which make her invincible for a short period—not only against enemies, but against Spikes. The only thing that *can* destroy you is if you're scrolled off the screen, so keep even your powered-up self from being caught between the right edge of a Ledge and the right side of the screen. By entering doorways that look like Game Boy units, Alice accesses bonus rounds. If Alice collects twenty Balloons there, a one-up Balloon will

appear. By pressing the B button, Alice can release
her Balloons, which is required now and then.
When she does, she has the ability to leap consider-
able distances using the A button and pressing up
on the pad. If you make Alice release them by mis-
take, you can undo the damage by jumping up
quickly and grabbing them again. If you wish, you
can also inflate a new Balloon by pressing the pad
down four times. Finally, you'll get a one-up for
completing a round, and another if you manage to
get every Balloon in the round.

Villains: There are two kinds of enemies: those that
simply destroy Balloons, and those that will try to
destroy Alice. Most of these are described in the instructions; the rest, like Caterpillars and Mosquitoes, are discussed below. As noted above, in
Hero, another villain is the moving screen itself: if
Alice gets pushed against one side and scrolled off,
she's a goner.

Points: Alice is awarded points for collecting Balloons,
including power-up Balloons. If she gathers 20 in
succession, double-point Double Balloons will arrive, accompanied by a musical fanfare. When powered-up, Alice gets 100 points each for any enemies
she slays.

Strategy: A general note: play in the horizontal center
of the screen so you can see what's coming from the
left; rise and fall as suggested below. In the bonus
rounds, hover over the Smokestacks and drop on
the Balloons if they start to collect in the air. Don't
hesitate to use the sides of the screen—if you're

headed in that direction and have to turn around, don't turn and try to accelerate. You'll be able to backtrack faster if you do like the wrestlers do when they throw themselves against the ropes: fling yourself against the side of the screen, and you'll bounce back to the other side.

Taking to the air, here's how to get Alice through the first five stages:

Stage One: Stay in the upper half of the screen until you've passed the Ledge with Spikes underneath. Drop to the lower half then, to avoid the Spikes on top. Go over the small Buildings, then stay low until the Bridge ends: rise quickly, because a Sparky is lurking on the Ledge to the left. Drop after that to avoid the Balloon popper above. When the Bridge appears below, wait until the enemy has passed and alight: the first Game Boy door is located there. When you emerge, walk along the Bridge: a power-up Balloon will rise from the water within moments. For nearly half a minute you'll be able to mow down every enemy in your way. Do so, but listen for the change in the music: it'll indicate that your power-up period is about to end. Stay high to avoid the Birds, dropping between them to grab Balloons when you can—it's okay if Alice touches them, but not her Balloon—then go over the next Building, drop down the alley on its left side, collect the Balloons, then release your Balloons and grab the one-up from beneath the next two Buildings. (Incidentally, if you die here, you'll go back a bit and be able to collect the one-up again: you won't gain any extra lives by doing so, but it's a great way to rack up a few octillion points.) You can reinflate here if you want, or you can simply leap to the next Bridge, using the Bird as a step stool—you'll just miss it if you try jumping on your own. Hop the

Burner Boys on the Bridge, drop down to the Island
beyond, and exit the stage.

Stage Two: Just follow the Balloon trail here, avoiding the Bees that come by just below the middle of
the screen, then drop *real* low over the first small
Island: there are Scorpions above who will crawl
down to the midpoint of the screen to try and pop
your transportation! You can get by them by slip-
ping past the first to the first Island, then past the
second to the second Island. Rise afterward and stay
in the middle of the screen, speeding between the
Scorpions ahead—there's one above and one below.
Stay low to avoid the one Scorpion beyond them, at
the top of the screen, then stay in the middle to get
by the Ledges above—killer Caterpillars lurk up
there. Maneuver to just above center after the second Caterpillar Ledge to avoid the swarm of Mosquitoes, then drop after the third Caterpillar Ledge
so that you're slightly above the Island below: Buzzy
Bee is up ahead, circling his Hive. Don't drop *too*
low, though, or Burner Boy will get you. Stay just
above the middle until after the next Mosquito
Swarm, then drop a bit to avoid another Bee. It's a
good idea, in fact, to release your Balloons now and
walk on the Island below; just make sure you jump
up to the lower of the two Ledges which will scroll
along soon, since there's a one-up on it! (Obviously,
you won't want to leap onto the uppermost Ledge:
Chow Chow is there, making unnerving sounds!)
You can, by the way, release your Balloons at the
one-up Ledge, grab it, then make a dash to the right
to try and grab the Balloons again; it's a tough maneuver, but it can be done. If you're walking, leap
the Chow Chow on the ground up ahead and get the
power-up Balloon that rises right beyond (sometimes before). Unless you inflate here, you'll have a

vast sea to leap: you can do it, though, if you hop onto the back of the Floppy Fish—you're powered-up and invincible, remember?—and jump to the Island beyond. There's another Island after that, and a towering Island next; you'll have to be airborne to reach it. A pair of Sparkies will fall right after you pass the high Island, so race ahead to avoid them . . . though if you get grounded here, it's no big deal. Then you can walk under the next Scorpion and inflate after you pass it. You'll have to gas up quickly, though: there's another super-tall Island beyond the pincered punk, and you can only reach it by flying. Once there, drop your Balloons on top and hop off the left side to get to another Game Boy door. Inflate quickly once inside and nab all the Balloons for a one-up. Once outside, stay just below the middle to avoid the Mosquitoes above and the Burner Boy below. After Burner Boy's Island, pull up to avoid the Mosquitoes. Stay high on the screen: Wacka Wacka Wolf is waiting for you below. When he's flush with the left side of the screen, rush over to that side, cut loose from your Balloons, and drop on his head. (The alignment with the left side will make sure you don't miss!) Grab the Balloons again —you'll bounce right off his head—hover over him, drop, and repeat. A total of four bops will do him in. If you happen to lose your Balloons, reinflate and keep going—you can pump up one if you land on his Island, just to get off and to one of the Ledges—or you can jump on him, Balloonless, from the Ledges on either side.

Stage Three: Take off at once or the Crabs will scuttle over and nail you. Once airborne, watch out for the Balloon Birds, which are more mobile than their non-Balloon counterparts and will pop your bubble fast. Stay high to avoid the first and second one, then drop fast to get away from the flock of Birds that covers all but the bottom of the screen. (If you're good, you can kick the Birds' Balloons and sink 'em . . . but don't try that unless you've tried the two-player game first.) When you pass under the Spiked Ledge—which is all along the top of the screen—watch for a power-up Balloon to rise from the sea; occasionally, a one-up will rise right after it. You'll have to do some fancy flying beyond this as Birds flit here and there; when you get by them, drop way down again to keep from colliding with another flock. There are more Birds, a high Island with Crabs, and then a very high Ledge with a one-up in it. Cut your Balloons loose, get it, and jump down to the Island when you emerge from the other side. Inflate and take off. If you can't inflate two Balloons here, take off with one, stop briefly on the Ledge in the sky and inflate there—but quickly, because that Ledge will fall. Get to the very top of the screen and fly over the next flock of Birds. You'll encounter a mass of Balloons after this, along with 500-point bonus Balloons hovering up and down up ahead. Beyond these, all you need do is fly into the Whale's mouth.

Stage Four: Die here and you get one continue, so at least *some* of the pressure's off. Walk across the Island—an Island in a Whale's mouth? Why not!?—and take off at the end, flying along just above the middle of the screen to avoid the giant's Teeth on top and the hopping Shrimp from below. Hover to the right of each, wait until it's on its way down, pass over it, hover, wait for the next one to descend, and so on. If one of them gets under you and bounces you up, you're going to hit a Tooth. Should that happen, try to get to one of the Islands below to reinflate. After the three Shrimp, you'll have a trio of Octopuses leaping up at you: employ the same tack here that you used with the Shrimp. There's a pair of Burner Boys beyond—with a nice little rest Island between them—after which . . . *slow down!* Two Teeth will fall in succession, and you'll be impaled if you don't watch your step. Trigger the first by standing under it—step to the right as it falls—and trigger the next one the same way, then continue. Go to the upper Ledge when you're past the Teeth, go to the left, cross to the right, ride the Ledge down, get the one-up, exit to the left, and ride that Ledge up. From there you can hop to the Game Boy door in the top left corner of the screen. The air ahead is thick with foes when you emerge: there's a Burner Boy in the middle of the screen, Shrimp to its left, a Flying Fish above, and another Burner Boy beyond. (You *can* go under the Burner Boys and avoid the Flying Fish, but that's a tough road to travel!) Stay to the top of the screen here and you'll be able to enter another Game Boy door. When you emerge, there are more Flying Fish, another Shrimp, another Burner Boy, and yet another Shrimp. You'll come to a safe Island afterward, and a Ledge: fly *under* the Ledge so you can get the power-up Balloon as soon as it emerges. If you fail to get it, you'll have a heck of a time with a layout similar to what you've passed through already . . . only *more* of it! The power-up should expire when you're near an Octopus with a Shrimp beyond it; clear them, and there's an island you can drop on to catch your breath. A few routine foes later and you'll reach a setup similar to what you faced at the end of Stage Two. Only this time the two Ledges border a giant Fish that pops out of the water and then submerges. You'll have to bop it when it's out, which'll be difficult to do unless you hover with the Balloons, let go, bounce off its head to a Ledge, and reinflate. You *can* hit it, bounce, grab the Balloons, and bounce a second time, but that tack will take a good deal of practice to pull off!

Stage Five: You start by leaving the Whale's mouth and having to fly through Rainstorms which push you down. Balloon Birds add to your woes here, followed by Lightning Bolts that spit Sparkies. These won't just pop your Balloon, they'll electrify Alice and send her into the drink. You've got to fly high to survive the Rain, and stay high between the Squalls so you're above the Sparkies. Each Bolt shoots just one Sparky, but it's usually followed by another one which sends a Sparky after you. So, if you can't get the altitude to ride the top of the Cloud (where you'll be safe), stay as high as you can for the first Bolt, drop down and speed under the Cloud, then rise to avoid the second. Watch it, though: if a Sparky strikes something, it can rebound and still zap you! After the Rain and Clouds, you'll encounter a plethora of Sparkies: navigate through them with the utmost care (no kidding!), but take heart—halfway through, a one-up will rise from the sea. You'll have to race through the next two Squalls: Birds are coming from the left, and you'll be pushed into them unless you get out of the Rain *pronto.* The pair of Squalls after that are easily negotiated, after which you can rest for a second on the Island. Walls of moving Sparkies are your next trial: pass through slowly, speeding up whenever there's an opening, putting on the brakes, waiting for the next opening, and so on; you'll be staying roughly one-third up the screen for most of this trip. There's an Island you can rest on, followed by more Sparkies, another Squall, and the end of the level.

The remaining levels are variations on everything you've done to this point. If you move through them slowly, watching what's coming at you, you'll have no trouble. One thing you should do in the later stages is alternate tapping to keep things slow: hit the A button to stay airborne, then tap the left side of the pad to inch forward. Repeat until you feel secure enough to speed ahead, then slow down again.

Rating: B

Gameplay is really novel in *Balloon Kid,* as far as Game Boy games go. The only drawback: after you've cleared the first two stages, the game *is* pretty much the same from stage to stage. Nonetheless, it's great entertainment for all ages, and a worthy addition to the Game Boy library.

BATMAN

Type: Shoot-'em-up on the land and in the air

Object: Armed with various weapons, Batman must make his way through the streets of Gotham City, the corridors of the Flugelheim Museum, the skies over the city, and finally the Gotham City Cathedral, in order to defeat the nefarious Joker.

Hero: Batman can leap or crouch, and at the start comes equipped with a gun (N): as he goes along, he can acquire stronger weapons by uncovering special Blocks. The Batwing has the ability to fly and fire from the front and back. Upon losing all your extra lives, you return to the first screen of that level, not necessarily the screen you were on. Remember: you can shoot through Walls with T. This is especially useful in the second Flugelheim level!

Villains: There are different kinds of criminals on the ground: some Thugs can simply walk and weaken Batman when they touch him; other Thugs can shoot; Cowboys can jump and shoot; and the various Tanks can jump, climb Staircases, and shoot. In the air, Planes can maneuver as described below.

Points: Players earn from a mere ten points for blasting Blocks, to 50 points for icing Thugs, to 300 points for destroying Planes, etc. No points are awarded for obtaining power-ups. If you die and start at the beginning of the level, you cannot reclaim all the power-ups, though you can blast the Blocks again for points.

Strategy: The fundamental attack-strategy to remember, wherever you are, is to shoot while crouching. Most enemy fire cannot get you in that position. Also, if you have one or more Batwings orbiting you, you can usually attack without being in any danger: simply stand on Walls overlooking your foes and let the Bats bash them to oblivion. The exception, of course, is when you face an enemy that can fire in ways other than parallel to the ground. Finally, when you're crouching and firing at a Tank, don't stand up just because it's been destroyed: any shots the Tank fired will still be headed your way! Note that in the following text, if we refer to one "Block" ahead or to the right or wherever, and you see many on your Game Boy screen, we're talking about the *dark-colored Block*—the one that contains a power-up. For the most part, we ignore the light-colored ones, which are only good for points. That said—to the batpoles!

Gotham City: Quickly race over the Drum, crouch and kill the Thug, wait until the next one comes into view on the right, blast him, then get onto the

Drum, jump up to the lowest Blocks, hop up to blast
the dark Block to the left, then jump over and collect the Spear Up. After you kill the next Thug, hop
onto the two Drums to wait for the Thug beyond to
turn his back, then plug him. Stay crouched and
wait for the Thug who'll be shooting at you. Blast
him, then hop onto the next two Drums, go up to
the Blocks on the left, hop up and shoot away the
Blocks above you to the right, claiming the Bonus.
Blast the Thug on the ground and continue. You'll
meet several more Thugs, all easily beaten if you
wait for them to turn their backs. (Not fair, but
then, who told them to be crooks?) When you come
to the set of four Blocks above you, shoot the two on
the left *only,* uncovering the Heart. When you jump
to grab it, you'll slam against the Blocks on the
right, which is fine: you'll land on the narrow Wall
at the bottom of the screen. When you do, jump up
at once to avoid the shooting Thug to the right of
the Pit. You need only jump once: the attacker will
march right into the Pit after firing! (You *knew*
these guys were dumb, but you had no idea *how*
dumb, right?) Now, you can stay on the bottom and
attack the Thug ahead. Ahead, stay off the overhead
Blocks and stick to the bottom. You'll come to a low
wall with two shooting Thugs guarding the other
side: wait until they're both marching to the right,
then blast them. Shoot the Blocks here to claim a
Batwing and a Faster Batwing. When you reach the
stack of seven Drums, get on top and jump to the
seven Blocks on top: the top two on the left contain
a W and a Heart. Skip the W (on the left) if you
don't like this weapon—it's powerful, but tougher to
aim. Jump to the Blocks on the right: the one on top
contains a B. Go to the Ledges along the top and
stay there, leaping from one small Ledge to another
(you're not missing out on much below: the Wall

with the Thug and three Blocks will only give you a B). When you come to the Blocks above the door, blast the ones on top, exposing the Faster Batwing, leap over, and shoot the Block on the left to uncover the Batwing. Drop to the ground and exit. (If you're using W, you can hit the Batwing first, in the lower Block, perched on the Blocks on the left.)

Axis Chemical Factory: Jump up and shoot the first Thug as he descends the Staircase, then cross the Vats, wait on the platform to the right of the rightmost Vat and shoot the two Thugs who come down the Staircase. At the top of the steps the dark Block ahead—the one with a Thug patrolling beneath it—has a B. Don't go up the next Staircase, but kill the two Thugs on the bottom when they're facing right and wriggle *under* the steps. Climb the Pipe, shoot the Thug on the other side, then blast the Blocks to get a B and a Batwing. There's a Tank on patrol beyond, so be ready to leap up and blast it. You'll find a Heart in the lowest Block up ahead—after two Vats, with a Thug patrolling beneath it. Slide down the right side of the Vat to the Pipe, wait for the Thug to walk right, then drop to the platform and plug him. Bust *all* the Blocks to clear a path so you can jump up to the next Vat. When the big Wall that splits the screen vertically appears on the right side, stay on the Catwalk you're on, hop up and shoot the Thug patrolling behind the Wall. Slide off the *left* side of that Catwalk, to the Catwalk below, shoot away the Blocks to get the Faster Batwing (top right); there's also an N in the block to its left if you want it. Keep shooting till the Thug on the other side expires. Go back up to the Catwalk above it, leap and kill the Thug to the right, get on his Catwalk, shoot the three Blocks to the right, and get the P from them—if you don't get all the Blocks,

the lower ones'll knock you into the Pit when you
jump over. When you leap to the next Catwalk,
make sure the Thug there is facing away from you.
Stay on the top Catwalks and plan your drop on the
two Thugs below so that you don't get shot. There's
a Spear Down in the top left Block on the bottom;
obviously, you'll want to avoid that. Get the S in the
next Block to the right if you want that weapon.
The Block in the upper right will give you a Heart;
shoot below it, in "thin air" beneath it—halfway
between the dark Block and the Catwalk—for a surprise. Leap to the next Catwalk, crouch, and shoot
the two Thugs. Continue right and get the B from
the Block there. At the Staircase leading down to
the right, crouch at the top and fire to the right to
destroy the Tank that's hopping up the steps.
There's a Smoke Bullet in the leftmost Block to the
right. The next Block—after the tall girderlike
Wall, by the two Vats—has a B. When you reach the
next Staircase, you'll have to shoot a Thug and
Tank in quick succession. The Block above the
double Staircase—where the Mini-Tank hops down
at you—contains an S. Two Mini-Tanks will rush up
the Staircase as you start down: blast them *or* hop
onto the Blocks to the right, get to the right of the
Mini-Tanks, face left and crouch, and blast them.
Get the B from the Block overhead. There's a Heart
in the top Block over the next Vat, and a Faster
Batwing in the Block to the right of the Vat.
Clearly, unless you're playing for points, whenever
you can get to the Catwalks at the very top of the
screen, it's a good idea to do so. You can avoid a lot
of trouble that way.

Axis Chemical Factory (Part Two): The second part
of the factory opens with a Tank attack. Proceed at
a crouch, destroying the first three, then get an S, if

you want, from the Block overhead. Another two Tanks will attack within moments as you head right, so move forward at a crouch, firing continuously. You'll find a B in the next group of Blocks, and the next Blocks will give you an N. At the edge of the Catwalk scope out the Tank below. Jump to the Pipe connecting the two Vats and crouch there, facing left. Rise and blast it when it's on the left. (While you're busy doing that, the Tank on the right will self-destruct by hopping into the Pit.) Get the B from the Block beyond. After the Vat, and under the Catwalk, jump down and get a Spear Up from the leftmost Block. If you just stay crouched here, the attacking Tank will leap over you and fall to its demise. (You *can*, instead, go up to the Catwalk, go right, then drop down and come left; your call.) After the Vat, hop onto the two vertically stacked Blocks and shoot at the Blocks to the right: the topmost has an R. Before leaping over, drop onto the Catwalk below you and take out the Tank patrolling to the right, then hop over and get the R. The Block at the end of the Catwalk where the Tank was rolling has a B; again, before jumping to the next Catwalk, destroy the tank there. When you reach the next high Wall—which has a small Catwalk in the middle where the Tank was rolling— blast the Blocks to the right: there's a Batman in the lower left Block. Jump for it when the Tank on the Catwalk beyond has turned to the right. That'll give you time to grab the one-up, land on the Catwalk, and fire before the Tank turns. Position yourself on the Blocks to the right to blow away the Tank on the next Catwalk. Get the Heart from the lowest Block, and skip the N in the Blocks to the left of the next Staircase. Go right to bring on the Mini-Tank, then rush to the left, crouch, and fire. You've got moving Catwalks to cross after that—with a B in the Block just before them, and a Batwing in the Block in their midst—so time your jumps. Watch for the Tank that'll attack you after you hop off the last one onto the Vat. There's a B in the Block to the right of the Vat, with another Tank attack. Cross the Catwalk, pause halfway down the Staircase to blast the Tanks on the Catwalk to the right, then continue down the steps to the Ledge. Jump up and fire at the Block to the right of the hanging Catwalk: there's a Batman in it. Don't try jumping for it: you'll perish. Instead, go to the foot of the Staircase, fire to the right, and uncover a helpful invisible Block. *Now* cross the Catwalk, and grab the Batman as you drop down onto the formerly invisible Block. On the other side of the Pit beyond is a Block with a Faster Batwing and a Tank below. Get on the Pipe to the right of the Vat and you'll have no trouble hitting the Tank. On the next Catwalk are two Tanks: get them when they're both headed right, then collect the B and Heart from the Blocks beyond. The next Block contains a Spear Down, so make sure you either leave it alone or blast the Blocks above it: you'll hate yourself if you hit them while trying to leap the Spear Down and land right on it!

Batman vs. Jack: Enter this round crouching and shooting. Whenever Jack nears, jump him, crouch, and open fire from the other side, keeping as much distance as possible between you and the villain. He's pretty easy to defeat!

Gotham City (Part Two): Shoot the Cowboy that attacks, then Spear Up in the first Block, hop the Pit, crouch on the right side of the wall, and fire at the three Cowboys who attack. There's a B in the Block overhead. Shoot the two Blocks to the right, to give you clear passage, then hop *quickly* across the four narrow Walls to the safe fifth Wall: Boulders will fall on the first four, so get off them fast—or else land on the far right side of the Wall, where they won't touch you. If you hop off a Wall and then back onto it after a Boulder has fallen, you'll still take a hit! However, once they've fallen, you can shoot Boulders away. You can also try blasting them as you go . . . tough, but fun! (Note: if you're *really* good, you can shoot the Tank to the right as you leap off the fourth Wall.) You're now in the inverted L of the Wall. Jump up, facing right, and shoot the Tank mentioned above. Then jump up, facing left, and destroy the Boulder. Hop onto that Wall, shoot the Block to the left, and get the Batwing. Jump back to the inverted L, then onto that Wall and up to the Ledge on the left. Hop up, shoot the Blocks, get the Batwing there—falling onto the Wall where you got the first Batwing—then get back onto the Ledge. Jump up, shooting the left two of the four Blocks in the upper right. Get the Faster Batwing, falling to the regular L-shape section of the Wall below. Hop onto the Ledge on the upper right. Another series of narrow Walls with falling Boulders follows: you can skip the first and jump right to the second; the third is safe, but the fourth contains a Block with a Spear Down in it, so don't uncover that. Instead, jump right from the second Wall *onto* those Blocks. When you clear the fourth Wall, you'll come to a short Wall to the left of a new Ledge. There are two Tanks on the Ledge, and you don't want to land in their midst; but if you land in the center of the Wall, you'll be hit by a falling Boulder. So, as with the narrow Walls, land on the Wall, but on its right side. The Boulder won't touch you there, and you can drop down when the Tanks are headed right—or just stand there and let them get whacked with Batwings, if you have 'em. The Block overhead contains an S. The next short Wall after the Pit offers a falling Boulder overhead and a Thug to the right; if you wait a moment before jumping, the Thug will march to the right and you can shoot him easily. Now, you can take Ledges along the top of the screen or stay on the bottom. You're better off taking the latter route, getting a Batwing from the Block ahead, crouching and shooting the Tank on the Wall to the right, then claiming the Faster Batwing in the next Block. In the Blocks above the next Wall, with its two Tanks, is a B. Leap to the narrow Wall on the right, hop up and shoot left, and get the B from the Block up there if you want it. Stay to the Catwalks on top if you want to avoid fighting, and get an R from the Block to the upper left of the next Pit. Jump the Pit, shoot at the Blocks across the next Pit (you'll get a B), climb the Wall, fire ahead at another bunch of Blocks for an N, *if* you want it— otherwise, don't uncover these Blocks—vault the Pit, get a P from the upper group of Blocks ahead, and stand there for a moment studying the multi-fire Cannon below to the right. When the Wall to its left is not under fire, drop down to it, shoot the Cannon, then get the B in the Block to the upper left. Stop on the Wall where the Cannon was and fire to the right: there's another Cannon just ahead, and shooting from here will destroy it. You'll find a B in the Block above it and Tanks patrolling on the next Catwalk. There's a Faster Batwing in the Block to the upper left of the Tanks in case you need it. Once you've destroyed the three Tanks here, get an S and a Batman from the Blocks directly overhead. Go to the right, careful not to scroll the Blocks at the top of the screen off to the left. Get on the uppermost of the two Blocks on the right, then hop left onto the Catwalk. Bust open the Blocks and take the Faster

Batwing. Go back down to the right and get a B from the Block you used to get up here.

Flugelheim Museum: (Note: this is incorrectly spelled *Flugalheim* on the screen!) Get an S from the first Block, then jump down and, staying to the left of the stubby Wall, pump Bat-lead into the two Thugs and Tank just beyond. Quickly jump onto the Ledge overhead if you don't want to battle the Tanks that'll come rolling along in a flash. There's an N after the next Thug, and a fast-shooting Thug on the other side of the Pit. Not only is the killer quick on the trigger, but the gun points whichever way you go! So dispatch the Thug before leaping the Pit—watch it, his fire reaches here—or get onto the Ledges and cross 'em quickly, outracing the bullets. Attack the next Thug by going past him to the Staircase on the right, turning, climbing down quickly—lest you be shot!—and firing to the left. There's a B here—which probably won't excite you too much at this point, eh? The lone Block over the next Catwalk contains a Spear Down. Don't uncover it, but use it to vault up to the overhead Catwalk if you want to face lots of Thugs and get a T from the first Block. Otherwise, take the low road, shoot enemies as they come along—easy here, since the corridor's so long—and collect the Faster Batwing at the end. (Frankly, we'd go for the T; it's one *mean* weapon that'll take out two Thugs with one shot. Just be careful when you shoot at Blocks, since it'll destroy *three* of them . . . not always a good thing!) Whichever way you went, get on top now, go to the right of the three Thugs marching below, shoot left to get rid of them, then get a Heart from the Block below. The next Block you'll encounter—on the bottom Catwalk—is a Batman. Continue ahead until you come to a row of Blocks with a Thug below and above to the right. Take out the top-right enemy first, then drop down and slay the other one. Blast all the Blocks and collect the Batman from the one on the bottom left. Press on and you'll reach a series of Columns: jump carefully from one to the other. Avoid, at all costs, the Blocks in their midst: you'll get an S, and it'll replace your seat-kicking T! There's a Heart in the Block at the other side.

Flugelheim Museum (Part Two): It's part two of the museum, and it begins with Cowboys on patrol. They're easy enough to destroy. You'll get a weapon in the first Block, a B in the second. Stay on the bottom: there's a trick floor above that'll drop you there anyway. (Once you learn where it is, you can jump over it. There are several fake floors in this level: if you're good, you can jump back up through them.) Even if you try to leap it, you're better off below. Proceed at a crouch, firing constantly, since Cowboys and Tanks are everywhere. When you reach the Staircase, the only way to go is up. At the Pit, drop to the very bottom—not to the middle level, since the Cowboys can fire up and get you here, while you can't fire down. After you cross the Column tops, you'll find Blocks tucked in a corner (two B's). Stay on the middle level here or you'll encounter an S and Spear Down, which'll rob you of the T . . . which, hopefully, you still have! There's an N in the set of Blocks just before the Staircase. Next, there are more moving Catwalks: you'll have to shoot the Door open from the last one, then jump through.

Batwing Stage: The patterns are always the same for this level, so that should help you after you get your head handed to you the first few times you play. The first attack comes from the right, so play just left of the halfway point, sweeping your Batwing up and down as you fire. Use a carpet-bombing technique: that is, lay it on thick, moving up and down so that the line of fire you're dropping seems to be a diagonal line. Do this whether you're firing front or rear. When the giant Chopper descends from the top center, stay with it as it comes down, keeping up your fire—otherwise it'll unleash a deadly attack. A few more Planes will attack from the right, after which the next wave comes from behind, the first few Planes attacking from the top. To beat them, fly with the top white "cloud line" passing through your Batwing, and just keep firing back. In general, for this wave, stay to the right of center. When the Planes start attacking top and bottom, repeat the diagonal-bombing technique. If you *do* get caught in a flurry of Bombs, now or at any point, try to fly *with* them; you can dodge them easier up and down if you're moving at the same speed as they are left and right. Three Choppers follow the wave of Planes from the left—all attack along the top; they arrive after two Planes fly in from the bottom—after which an assortment of aircraft arrive. Continue shooting *backward* from this location—with that white cloud line passing through you, your Batwing just to the left of the score—during the next Chopper/Plane wave; if you let these new Choppers get to the right of the screen, the air'll be so thick with Bombs, you're sure to suffer some hits. Inch to the right *ever so slightly* when the mini-Choppers rise from above, all the while keeping up your backward gunning. Shift to forward-firing immediately when the egglike aircraft arrive. When the Missiles start rising from below, you can drop to the very bottom of the screen and pick them off or shoot them from whichever side you're on. The problem with the latter tack is that they'll start to shift, diagonally, to where you are; after you've shot down five or six of them, race to the other side and continue firing from the opposite direction. Otherwise, they'll box you in a corner. After the Missiles, Planes will attack from behind—with a couple of easy-to-defeat Missiles rising from below—stay in the center of the screen, so you don't get caught by the latter. After these, more Missiles will attack from the front (flying horizontally). The new Missiles don't shoot at you, nor are they particularly fast. Consider it a brief respite: after they leave, it's time for the Boss.

The Boss, here, is a squarish ship, and begins spitting Bombs in all directions shortly after it arrives. After the Missile wave, stay to the left of the screen, on the bottom, and shoot toward the right. Stay on the left: the Boss will rise and dart right to the right. If you're in the way: *crash!* When it returns, circle it once, counterclockwise, and get on the right side, bottom. Dodge its Bombs by dropping to the middle, then to the bottom for the next wave, then rising. In any case, stay as far from the Boss as possible, since you'll need room to maneuver. Whatever you do, *don't* try to weave between the Bombs: they're too close together for that. After each flurry of Boss Bombs, resume your fire at the machine's center. Just remember, the Boss is tenacious: it'll try and follow you wherever you go, meaning you have to stay on the move.

Batwing Stage (Part Two): The second part is more of the same—for about two seconds! After the first wave from the right, you'll have to dodge the deadly, scrolling Clouds . . . after which, shift at once into backward-fire to deal with some bizarre X-wing craft. When they're dispatched, you'll be attacked from *both* sides. *Stay dead center,* firing from both front and back while bobbing and weaving only as much as necessary. When the egg-shaped ships arrive from the right, go to the far right of the screen and shoot them the instant they emerge. Then back off: the next wave of ships turns into Bombs when destroyed! The first Boss, this time, is a Plane: big and Bomb-spitting. It'll enter from the left, and when it shows up, get to the left of it, riding up and down as it does, ducking its fire while you keep up an offense of your own. P.S.: don't think you've won when the Plane sinks off the bottom of the screen. Like the shark in *Jaws*, it's gonna come right up under you! In other words—when it goes down, you go up! When it returns, stay on the left side of the screen and fire at it while rising slowly up and down: you'll be able to weave through its fire. It's followed by a deadly Chopper which comes from the left: open fire before it arrives, midscreen. The Chopper erects a wall of Bombs which peel off at you from the top. Simply rise as the first one comes at you, go over it, move to the right, and come down on the other side of the Bomb Wall, easily avoiding the rest.

Only skill is going to get you farther than this, skill plus looking for invisible Blocks—look for sets of invisible Blocks to get you across some long gaps in the first Cathedral level—and be ready to react *fast* in the second Cathedral level since the game scrolls by itself. You would do well to have the Wave Weapon (W) here to attack foes lurking behind and around objects.

Rating: B

If you liked *Super Mario Land,* you'll like *Batman.* This game's a little easier, and the enemies aren't as diverse, but you'll have a good time. You can continue as often as you want, but as stated above, you'll be booted back to the beginning of the entire level.

BOOMER'S ADVENTURE IN AZMIK WORLD

Type: Fantasy quest

Object: The perpetual peace and sunshine of Azmik World is destroyed one day by the arrival of Lord Zoozoon and his dark tower. Bent on conquering Azmik, Zoozoon can only be stopped if an Azmikian is brave enough to enter the tower, overcome its dangers, and confront the evil lord himself. Boomer is such a hero!

Hero: In his natural, unadorned state, Boomer has the ability to walk and dig Holes. Doing the latter, the reptilian hero is able to uncover various weapons as described in the instructions. All, including the Key, are usually found in the same place from game to game. (If they're not, it's because somebody stole 'em!) Boomer can also pick up any power-ups he finds lying around. The drawback is that some weapon he picks up supplants whatever he had before that—meaning if he acquires a Compass and suddenly goes for a weapon to get out of a jam, it's bye-bye Compass. (Eggs, however, are not lost

once acquired . . . unless, of course, Boomer dies!)
Boomer has the power to walk over enemies who
have been dumped into Holes. However, if they're
just about to get out and he falls in, he's doomed.
Lastly, this has nothing to do with strategy, but
watch the Compass *spin* when you use it directly
atop a Key!

Villains: These are pictured in the instructions. Most
roam the screen; a few, like Bouncer and Zoozoon,
don't move until five seconds after the stage has begun. Beware, though: they can grab things you need
and move them around—including a Key! So take it
as soon as you've spotted or uncovered it, or kill the
thing that stole it!

Points: You get no points for picking up weapons or
power-ups other than the Key—which gives you five
hundred points. Points are awarded for killing foes,
starting at 20 points for a mere Creepy.

Strategy: You can't get any codes until you reach the
first Boss . . . but here are a few tips.

> *Stage One:* If you can't get through this,
> don't bother playing.
> *Stage Two:* Get the Compass below—or sim-
> ply go right, to the Wall equal with the top of
> the Compass room, and dig over the Wall
> that's above it.
> *Stage Three:* Head down, right, up, and left.
> You'll find the Key in the vertical passageway
> to the left above the Wall over your starting
> place.

Stage Four: Pick up the Detector, head right, and use it to find the Compass—below your starting room, to the right. Or simply go to the bottom right of the screen, stand facing left, and dig to get the Key.

Stage Five: You'll find the Key on the left in the center. Go inside the Wall that looks like the top half of a 7 and dig in the upper right corner.

Stage Six: Don't get the Compass first, even though it's right in front of you. Go for the Bone to the right of it and destroy Barfy first. (Which Barfy? The one above you . . . which is where the Key is buried!)

You get the drift of the game. However, if you're a seasoned player looking for some help in getting further, here are some codes—obviously created by a zoology buff:

Stage Eight: SCARAB and AXOLOTL give you different sections to think about!

Stage Nine: BLUTEN transports you here. Pick up the Detector and walk to the lower left for a Compass . . . or, if you want, grab the Boomerang on the left and make your way down, killing Barfys. More than likely, one of them has the Key.

Stage Ten: Go to the upper center on the right, to the Walls shaped like a W. You can usually get a Detector there—below the two center Walls—or you can blast one of the local Crawlers for a Compass.

Stage 11: Good news! You'll find Roller Skates to start things off, and they'll be *most* helpful.

Stage 15: REMORA zips you here.

Stage 16: PANGOLIN or CHIMERA are the codes.

Stage 17: The magic word is DEWLAP.

Stage 23: Use MINORCA to go here.

Stage 24: ELYTRON is the word.

Stage 25: GILA will get you to this monster of a level. There, try this, which works *sometimes*. From the starting place go up, left, down, right, up around the Wall, down, and right. Face right and dig for the Key. Not there, you say? Aha! Wait until Flippy arrives. The slug will fall in and frequently give you the Key. Take it and run! If that fails, keep going down and to the left for a Snow Cone. Below it, kick butt to get the Compass. There's another Snow Cone to the lower right.

Stage 26: Go to the bottom right side for enough Eggs to last several lifetimes.

Stage 32: HYDRA is your ticket up to this level.

Stage 33: IBEX really drops you in the thick of things. When you get here, go straight and stand on the first batch of Bricks, dig a Hole ahead of you, get the Bomb—taking care not to fall into the Hole, or you're dead—detonate it slightly to the right (making sure you're out of range of its blast—though Zoozoon can be hurt by it), and use the Roller Skates and Boomerang there to attack the tyrant. To get to the tower top and start your descent, use the code JEDOCH.

Finally, if you simply want some experience battling Bouncer, input ZAHNBELA. Dig up the Boomerang right in front of you and go to work!

Rating: B

Fans of fast-paced action games will be disappointed by the relatively slow pace of the game and the endless running from foes. But the "search for buried treasure" aspect is enjoyable, and the diversity of weapons keeps things lively.

BOXXLE

Type: Maze-type puzzle

Object: In order to impress the girl of his dreams, Wally the warehouse worker is working overtime! He's shifting crates around . . . and you have to help him move them into place in the fewest number of steps possible.

Hero: Wally can push crates in any direction, but he cannot *pull* them. Once a Crate is pushed into a corner, or against another Crate, it can't be removed.

Villains: The crates and walls are your passive foes.

Points: You're charged a "step" every time you move. Your task is to amass as few of these steps as possible.

Strategy: Rather than go through all 108 screens—
you'd be bored, and there'd be no room for any
games except for this one—here are the passwords
to bring you to each level:

1. BDBD
2. DBBD
3. GBBG
4. HBBH
5. JBBJ
6. KBBK
7. LBBL
8. MBBM
9. NBBN
10. PBBP
11. QBBQ

However, to give you a taste of what it's like to
triumph over real *Boxxle* adversity, here's how to
beat the toughest screen, 11–08: push the top Crate
to the upper right dot, and the bottom Crate to the
bottom right dot. Go to the two Crates side by side
on the left and push the right one so it's under the
left one. Go back to the two Crates on the dots and
push them each to the *left* dots—upper left and
lower left, respectively. Go to the lower Crate on the
right and push it to the left one —so it's to the lower
left of the one above it, forming a horizontal stack.
Get under the lower left Crate and push it up one.
You now have a horizontal stack. Move the one on
the right down one. Shove the Crate to your left
onto the top right dot. So far, you've filled the top
two dots, and the one on the bottom left. Now, move
the Crate on the lower right so that it's just to the
right of the center dot. Return to the Crate on the
lower left dot and push it three steps to the right, so
that it's diagonally below and to the right of the
Crate you moved in the previous step—that is, the
Crate to the right of the center dot. Go to the stack

on the left and move the top Crate to the middle dot on the left. Go to the Crate in the lower right and push it to the left one—so you've formed a stack of two. Push the Crate above it to the left one, onto the center right dot. The four top dots are now covered. Move the Crate on the right up one, move the Crate on the left five spaces—so it's diagonal to the one you moved in the previous step, below it, to the right—then go around the lowest Crate and push it to the left bottom dot. Push the last remaining Crate onto the last dot. The password will be QB8L.

Rating: B—
Sure, it's tough and fun to figure out some of these puzzles . . . but for all its challenges, *Boxxle* lacks the wonderful, frantic urgency of *Dr. Mario* or *Tetris*, while all the walking 'round isn't as convenient as the "helping hand" that lets you move pieces in *Daedalian Opus*.

BUGS BUNNY CRAZY CASTLE

Type: Maze chase

Object: Bugs's beloved Honey Bunny has been spirited away. She's being held in Crazy Castle and, to rescue her, Bugs must collect Carrots and battle various "Rascals."

Hero: Bugs is pretty stripped down compared to his cartoon persona. He can walk, climb Staircases, wriggle through Pipes, and push objects over on foes. When Bugs drinks Carrot Juice, he can destroy any adversary simply by walking on him. Bugs has another unannounced but interesting power: if he passes through a Pipe at the same time as a bad guy, the Wabbit won't be wounded! Another splendid if bizarre power: if Bugs faces a Wall, the nearest bad dude will almost always walk away!

Villains: The usual array of Warner Brothers baddies: Daffy Duck, Yosemite Sam, Sylvester, and Wile E. Coyote—do you think they could spell his name correctly in the instruction booklet?

Points: Carrots are worth 100 points each; not bad, eh, Doc? Bopping a Puddy Tat or other nemesis earns from 100 to 500 points, depending on how it's done —a Carrot Juice clobber gets less than a Boxing Glove bash!

Strategy: The levels are self-explanatory; herewith are the first 20 passwords with a few tips, and significant codes to get to levels beyond:

Two: SZWS
Three: ZS2S
Four: ZZPS
Five: SW3S
Six: SXES (You don't need the Bucket to win on this level.)
Seven: ZW4S
Eight: ZX9S (You'll get Magic Carrot Juice here for the first time.)
Nine: WSRS
Ten: WZFS (Don't do the section near you first, but go right and do the next section over. Otherwise, a pair of Sylvesters will trap you on the Walled middle level there when you get to it. When you're done there, go back to the left section.)
Eleven: XSJS
Twelve: XZKS
Thirteen: WWMS (Be careful, here: the Rascals aren't going to walk blindly into whatever you push off a Ledge! They'll stop or turn around.)
Fourteen: WXCS (You'll have to do a bit more walking than usual to get around all the Walls.)
Fifteen: XWAS (Forget the Carrots: go down and get the Boxing Glove first, then go back up

and get the Carrots. Without the Glove, Sylvester will corner you.)

Sixteen: XXOS (Sometime during the round you'll have to get the Boxing Glove from the top middle, so work your way toward it.)

Seventeen: S2SZ (Go to the bottom first, but save the Boxing Glove for the tenacious Daffy on the middle floor. Or, if you can sneak by him, bop him with the Bucket above!)

Eighteen: STWZ

Nineteen: Z22Z

Twenty: ZTPZ

Thirty: WYCZ

Forty: TX9W

Fifty: 2TWX

Sixty: YTKX

Seventy: SHE2

Eighty: XH02 (Plan to stay behind objects, pushing them, as much as possible. Running down your opponents is the only way you're going to get through this. When you win here, you can accept "congraturations" from Bugs. Yes, you read it right. The gamemakers should be ashamed of that. And no, it's not "Bugs talk" : the entire phrase was written by someone with only a passing knowledge of English. Boo!)

You may not have noticed, but—the passwords are the same as in the NES version! Check our book *How to Win at Nintendo Games 3* for a complete rundown.

Rating: B
A delight for kids, and a pleasant diversion for everyone else . . . though experienced videogamers will get through the entire game in about an hour!

THE CASTLEVANIA ADVENTURE

Type: Fantasy quest

Object: If you've played the NES versions of this game, you know what it's all about! You're off to see Count Dracula by making your way through four levels of evil danger. The land can only be cleansed when you've met and destroyed the fang-tastic vampire.

Hero: You make your way through the game armed with a Mystic Whip. As you proceed, it's essential that you light—that is, whip—Candles, some of which will give you power-ups described in the instructions. Of these, Crystals are most important, for they give you a super-long Whip (first Crystal) and Fireball power (second Crystal). Crosses are good too, but the invincibility they bestow only lasts for six seconds. Generous, huh? The hero's only other powers are his ability to jump, crouch, and climb Ropes . . . the last of which will prove surprisingly important!

Villains: These are pictured in the instructions, and are discussed below.

Points: Everything you kill swells your total—starting at 20 points for lowly monsters (you earn the same amount, by the way, if you destroy them whether they're forming or already formed . . . so you might as well get them before they're a danger!)— and everything you collect also earns you points (not to mention power), beginning with ten points for a Heart. While all this whipping is going on, you're playing against the clock, so don't dawdle! You don't get points for monsters that die of their own doing, such as rolling into a pit—for example, the Big Eyes on the Bridge in Stage Two.

Strategy: Here we go, traipsing stage by stage through the land of the sanguinary Count.

Stage One: Don't light the first Candle. Pass it right by, but whip all the rest and kill all the enemies; easy stuff. Climb the Rope and head left: make sure you get the Candle above the second step. Because you skipped the first Candle, this one will give you a one-up! After you climb the second Rope, the sluggards here come at you twice, so don't just stroll ahead after you've hit 'em once, expecting they'll go away—a lengthened Whip or Fireballs will stop them in their tracks, though. The third Rope will lead you right into eyeball country: beware the Big Eyes rolling at you down the Staircase to the left; after you go up the next Rope, they'll be attacking from the right. The Crosses you find here will help you get through. When you climb the next Rope— the one with the Tree Trunk to the left—don't stop at the top, but keep going through the roof! There's a horde of Candles up there, one of which will give you a one-up. Die on purpose after coming down, and you can collect another two one-ups . . . not a bad trade! When you climb the next Rope (on the left), jump off and whip the Candle on your way down. It'll give you a Heart. (You can get the next Candle over only if you've gotten enough Crystals to give you a Fireball Whip. It's worth getting: there's a one-up inside!) When you reach the Ledges on the right, hop from one to the other as fast as your sinews can carry you: they fall as soon as you set foot on them. The Candle on the other side has a Heart —whip it from the right side. Beyond are skinny Ledges; go below them to collect the power-ups from the Candles, then return to the left to cross the Ledges. It'll be a big-time help if you have Fireballs to deal with the Bats as you hop along. Anyway, if you leap and whip as you land on each Ledge— never letting the Bats in too close—you'll be okay. (Hint: take your hops from the right edge of each Ledge, with your right foot actually off the side, or you won't make it.) The long Ledges at the end of the second group of narrow Ledges falls like the first bunch did. After getting through, it's time to tango with Gobanz. Remain on top of the Ledges prior to his arrival; otherwise, you'll have problems. To defeat Gobanz, you've got to stay behind him and his wrought-iron spear—unless you've got Fireballs, in which case it doesn't much matter.

Stage Two: The first Candle is a Cross; get it by *hurrying* to the fourth Column, turning to the left, whipping the trio of Bats that attack, then leaping high to the left to hit the Candle. The second Candle is a Crystal. Another leathery threesome follows— no problem if you got the Cross—after which you'll

obtain a Crystal from the Candle and confront a
Fireball-breathing Punaguchi. The creature's flam-
ing projectiles ricochet around the chamber *and*
survive its death, but at least you can Whip them. If
you have Fireball power, scroll the monster into
view, then crouch against the right side of the Column to the left of the flamester and just keep shooting. If you aren't equipped with Fireballs, stand
with your back just to the right of the left Candle—
the Fireball won't get you there—destroy Punaguchi at your leisure, then smash the Fireball.
There's another Punaguchi a few paces beyond—
nestle next to the Column it's on, and the Fireballs
won't get you—and a third after that, hanging upside-down. You'll meet its Fireballs before you see it,
so be on your guard: stand on the edge of the Column you'll have reached when the Fireballs start,
whip the first one, then rush ahead. Attack the
Punaguchi on top, whipping all the Candles to get
the Hearts, then drop off the Ledge. There's a Zeldo
below: it's recommended that you avoid it by climbing down the Rope between its Boomerang tosses. If
you're intent on killing it, walk left and duck the
Boomerangs when they're thrown, leap them on
their way back, and continually get closer until you
can whip the sucker. Three lashes will do it, but be
careful: the Boomerangs also survive Zeldo's death!
Collect the Candles to the left, then turn right—and
you'll have to fight Zeldo again! (See why we said to
avoid this dude?) When you kill him, head to the
Rope, descend, and jump *at once,* facing left and
whipping: if you stand in that little depression, a
Punaguchi Fireball will nail you. Destroy the Fireball, then rush forward. Whip the next Fireball as it
emerges, then plug Punaguchi. Step on the Ledge
just beyond. It'll fall; hop off to the Ledge on the
right as it does. You'll get a much-needed Heart

from the Candle on the right. Climb down the Rope
on the right, get the Crystal from the Candle to the
left, whipping it as you leap and grabbing it as you
land on the falling Ledge. Take a few steps before
you leap to the next falling Ledge, then take another few steps to jump to the Column. Climb down
the Rope, whip the Fireball to the right, and charge
the Punaguchi. Jump off the Ledge between Fireballs from the Punaguchi below, deep-six that one,
descend the Rope, and cross the Bridges. Jump the
Big Eyes here, or whip them when they're to your
left: if you kill them on your right, their explosive
deaths will leave gaping holes in the Bridge! Not an
insurmountable problem, since you can jump them
. . . but why bother? Whip one behind you, though,
and those to your rear will fall in the hole. (Remember, if you only have a normal Whip, you have to
crouch to beat these 'orrible orbs.) The first Candle
after the Bridges contains a welcome Heart. (Note:
if you die at any point here, you'll be resurrected at
the first Bridge instead of going all the way back to
the beginning.) Climb down the Rope and you'll
come to falling Ledges: cross them to the Candle on
the left, claim the one-up, then get the Candles below (Coins in both) and climb down the Rope on the
right: the right Candle below has a Cross. If you
hurry to it, the Bats won't hurt you until you get it.
Go down the left Rope and descend the Columns.
Stand on the lowest, rightmost Column *facing left*:
whip a Big Eye when it's on that Column to your
left, and its death will open a doorway in the Column. (If you hit it when it's too far to the right, only
a partial doorway will open. Wait for another Big
Eye to come along and repeat.) Descend for a Heart,
Coin, Crystal, and one-up. (Just be careful a Big Eye
doesn't roll in after you: you can be hurt while
you're descending!) Climb down the Rope, deal with

the Punaguchi below by dropping down when the
Fireball is headed right for the first time. Climb
down the Rope, cross the room to the next Rope, and
fight your old friend Zeldo by waiting until the first
Boomerang has been tossed, then crouching near
the base of the step and whipping the Boomeranger
as it approaches. (Note: if you die from this point
forward, you'll return here rather than at the beginning of the round.) The second Candle has a
Crystal; another Zeldo attacks just after the third
Candle. Climb down the Rope at the end and face
the boss—bosses, actually, as a slew of Under Moles
leap from their holes to pounce on you. Watch
where they're coming from: if they come from the
rightmost Hole (number one), stand just to the right
of the next Hole (number two) facing right; if they
emerge from number two, stand beneath that Hole
and face left; if they hop from number three, stand
beneath it and face right; and if it attacks from the
leftmost Hole (number four), position yourself just
slightly to the left of the third Hole facing right.
Never let the creatures collect or they'll overwhelm
you.

Stage Three: The first two Candles are gifts: they're
only Coins, but they're easy to get. After that you
can't just jump at 'em with impunity: if you touch
the Spikes in the ceiling, you die. For the third Candle, jump at it from the second step rather than
from the top of the Staircase; it's a Crystal. The second Candle beyond—after the high Wall you're on—
is a one-up: if you don't have Fireballs, you can still
get it; we'll tell you how in a moment. Get the
nearer Candle by whipping it and catching it on the
ground, and continue right. When the ceiling starts
to descend, it's because there's a giant Screw up
ahead: run to it and Whip it four times to make it

vanish. When it goes, the roof will rise again. Turn quickly to the left and rush to the one-up Candle before it rises, and you'll be able to whip it. (Obviously, the lower you let the roof come, the lower the Candle will be when you go back for it.) You'll have to get rid of the Screw again, but that's no big deal. Beyond the Screw, *crouch* in the Spiked niche ahead when the ceiling comes down and wait for it to go up before continuing. Whip the next Screw and hurry ahead; the ceiling is "stepped," and you have to get under the highest of these steps and crouch— it's as high as the last Spiked niche you curled up in. If you pause to light the Candles, you won't have enough time to get to safety no matter *how* fast you are. We suggest you get to the niche and go *back* for the Candles—a Coin in the leftmost Candle, a Heart in the nearer one—then get in the niche again when the roof comes down. *Don't* try to get them then go onward without pausing in the niche: you'll need all the time you can muster to deal with the Screw twisting up ahead. There's a Crystal in the Candle beyond, and the infamous collapsing Ledges follow. When you get to the Ropes, climb *fast*: the floor will rise, and it's covered with deadly Spikes! (If you die here, this is where you'll be reincarnated.) Get on the one on the left, climb, and transfer to the Rope on the right as soon as the Spikes are just about to touch the Rope you're on— you'll fall when you jump for the Rope on the right, but fear not: you'll catch it in time. When you reach the Ledge, you'll notice the big, ugly She Worm to the right: hop off the Rope before she comes all the way over—you can't afford to wait for her to head left, the floor will have risen by then—whip the Worm, leap it or Whip it when it turns into a ball and rolls at you—which it'll do if you use a normal Whip; anything else will kill it on the first shot—

then get to the next Rope and continue up. See the Worm to the right on the Ledge? Drop off the Rope when it's headed right—you can afford to wait for that to happen here. Whip it, hop it, then climb the next Rope. (You can't stay on the Rope you were climbing: it ends and there's nowhere to go!) Climb the Rope as high as you can and drop down to the collapsing Ledges, cross them—with the floor still rising beneath your fast-moving feet—grab the rightmost of the Ropes on the left, climb, transfer to the leftmost of the Ropes on the left (got that?), repeat the procedure with the Worm, then climb . . . but get off the next Rope quickly so you can cross the Ledge before the Spikes arrive. The next Rope looks like it might lead you to safety . . . but it doesn't. It leads you to a Ledge that blocks the way. So get off onto the Ledge on the left when you can, *hurry* across it—those Spikes'll be tickling your tootsies by now—and take the next Rope up. There will be a Staircase to the right with She Worms on each of the two upper steps: take them out from the step below, then scurry up the Rope on the right. Do a Tarzan and switch to the one on the left when you can, head to the Ledge on the left, and climb the Rope above. When you reach the Ledge, don't jump to it. You'll die here, since there's no way off on the right side. Instead, you'll have to hop onto the narrow Ledge above, jump from it to another narrow Ledge—as you did in Stage One, edge to the far right of the Ledge—then race across more collapsing Ledges. You can actually make it from the last Ledge to the Rope without hopping onto the outcropping of Wall on the right . . . something that'll save you a few precious seconds. (If you fall off one of the narrow Ledges, you'll have just enough time to get back on the Rope, climb, and try it again *once*. Frankly, it'd be more fun having your gums tattooed than going through this section!) Ascend the Rope. There's a narrow Ledge to the left: go high enough on the Rope to jump onto it, Whip the Worm, and continue up. (If you try climbing the Rope instead, you'll get nowhere . . . except to a dead end. And we *do* mean dead!) A few more Ropes and then—phew!—the Spikes stop rising. Instead they start rolling from the right. There are a number of important Candles here, but you'd be unwise to stop and get them unless the Spikes are more than two-thirds of the screen behind the Candle. After all the Spikes have come and gone, you'll come to a screen which is mostly Wall with a Rope running up the left side. Just above the midway point let go of the Rope and jump right: you'll pass through the Wall and enter a bonus room. The Rope on the left is your passage out. The boss is a Death Bat who, like most bosses, should be attacked from behind. Just stay out of the monster's way when it's flitting around the room, then sneak into position before it alights. You'll have an easier time by far with this bat, man, than you did with the Moles in the last level!

Stage Four: Whip the Candles as you cross the room, but watch out for the Armor: some of it's Evil Armor, and it'll attack. After this it's déjà vu: there's a Zeldo at the end of the room, after which you must fight a Gobanz and some Punaguchis. There's nothing hereafter you haven't faced before, though there are some ugly new twists. For example: Ledges with Spikes above them which force you to take low, careful jumps; individual Spikes that jut from a wall of Spikes and must be used as Ledges—you have to land on them while avoiding the sharp tips right next to them—and, of course, Count Dracula himself. Before battling the vampire, you'll be able to engage in a secret power-up: there's a room patrolled by a Zeldo, with a Rope coming up from the left, and another poking down from the right. When you get past the Boomeranger and are on your way up the Rope on the right, climb until you're nearly halfway up and then leap off the Rope to the left. Just jump off: there's an invisible Ledge here and it'll enable you to walk parallel to the ceiling, just below it. When you reach the midpoint under the roof, hop up and climb right into it. There's a bonus room beyond! As for the Count, when you reach his chamber you'll notice that there are many Ledges. Unlike previous rooms, Ledges don't automatically give you sanctuary. He can get you on most of them. To fight him, stay on the left side of the Wall, hanging off the edge, when Dracula appears on the Ledge in the ten o'clock position. He'll shoot at you diagonally three times, miss, then fire parallel to the floor. When he does this, jump up and blast him on his right side. After firing thrice again, the vampire will vanish and reappear on the right side of the screen, on the Ledge in the two o'clock position. Reverse the tactic—hang off the right side of the Wall—and repeat. Drac'll quickly tire of the left/right attack and materialize at the top of the screen. Go to the Ledge on the far left or right bottom to avoid his fire, and get up on the Ledges he was on before to shoot at him if you can. After a brief stay on the top, the Count will come to the bottom: though you *can* hit him by getting on the uppermost Ledges and jumping down to shoot when the coast is clear, it's suggested that you simply avoid his fire until he goes back to the left and right. When he does, renew your attack as described above. After you've given the vampire a bit of a pounding, he'll transform himself into a giant Bat who swoops back and forth. Using the Ledges that

Dracula was on—at the ten and two o'clock positions—blast him when he's near . . . and especially when he pauses in his flight to disgorge smaller Bats. He won't be paying attention to you then, and is particularly vulnerable. Beat the Bat and you've won the game!

Rating: A

This was one of the earliest Game Boy games, and it's still one of the best. A marvelous adaptation of the NES game, with an endless variety of challenges and impressive music and sound effects. As quest games go, it's tough to beat . . . in every sense of the word!

CATRAP

Type: Maze game

Object: Catboy and Catgirl are lost in the Forbidden Area, a region of Monsters. Annoyed at being disturbed by the intruders, the creatures turn them into humanoid cats: the only way the curse can be eliminated is for Catboy and Catgirl to make it all the way through the many labyrinthine rooms.

Hero: Catboy can climb, leap, walk, retract moves, bust down certain Walls, punch out Monsters, and move Stones. Stones cannot be budged, however, if they're accidentally placed side by side.

Villains: Monsters sit still or hover; they don't attack.

Points: None. You race against the clock, trying to make the best time possible. There's no penalty for "taking too long."

Strategy: Each room is different; here's how to get through some of them. The first two rounds are simple. Here's help for what follows:

> *Round Three:* On the left side, go down the Ladder first and push the lower Stone to the right before pushing off the top Stone.
>
> *Round Four:* Smash the Wall under the Stone to move it.
>
> *Round Five:* Smash the Wall under the Monsters on the right, climb the Ladder, drop onto the Ledge in the upper left, bash just *one* section of Wall—under the Monster on the right—clobber the creature when it falls, then finish off the Ledge. The rest is easy.
>
> *Round Six:* Stand on the head of the Monster in the bottom left to reach the one on top. Hit the Monster on the bottom right to drop the Stones; the rest is easy.
>
> *Round Seven:* Push the top Stone twice to the right. Go under it by hanging onto the Mini-Ladders, get on the Stone's right side and push it left. Use the same Mini-Ladder to drop onto the Monster below.
>
> *Round Eight:* Push the bottom Stone left, then climb and push the top Stone right—so it falls on the bottom one. Get on top of it and sock away!
>
> *Round Nine:* Smash the Walls under the two Stones, but stand *under* the Stone on the left so it doesn't fall. While standing there, kick the Stone on the right further to the right. Then take a step right and let the Stone fall. Place one atop the other to get the Monster.
>
> *Round Ten:* Use the Mini-Ladders to get yourself to the left of the Stone without mov-

ing it. Drop left and smash the bottom section of the Wall before going around and pushing the Stone over. Bust the Wall on top of the fallen Stone, go around it, and push the Stone over to get the Monster.

Round 11: Walk under the Monster and the Stone, smashing the Wall as you head left. Let the Stone fall, then go around the room counterclockwise to get on top of it and pummel the creature.

Round 12: Go up the Ladder and push the top Stone to the right, into the gap. Continue to the right, down the Ladder, and push the Stone in the lower right to the left, into that gap. Head back up the Ladder, walk left, climb down the Ladder on the left, knock away the Wall under the Stones, and push the lowest Stone into the gap to the right. Shove the last Stone off the Ledge and then just drop down to push it into place. The Monster is yours!

Round 13: Knock the Stone on the right into the gap past the Mini-Ladder, then climb down that Ladder to dig up the Wall to the left. Climb the big Ladder to the right, push off the *top* Stone, shove the Stone below it so that it's now on top of it, then bop the Monster. Go down the Ladder, push the lowest of the two stacked Stones into the gap, move the remaining Stone into the last gap, then hit the creature there.

Round 14: Go over the heads of the Monsters and push the top Stone once to the right. Walk under each monster in turn, cutting away the Wall, stepping left to drop the Monster above, punching it out, and repeating. When only the Monster between the Stones remains, get rid of the Wall beneath the Stone on

the left, step to the right to let it drop—you're
now under the last Monster—push the Stone
left and finish the level.

Round 15: Climb the Ladder, drop from the
Mini-Ladders to the Stone on the right Ledge,
push it into the Pit, climb the Ladder again,
push the top Stone so it's resting atop the last
Mini-Ladder on the left, drop down to the
Stone below it and push that one to the right,
into the Pit so it's right on top of the other
Stone. Drop onto it and eat through the Wall to
the right. Go up the Ladder once again and
drop to the Ledge atop the remaining section
of destructible Wall. Climb the Ladder on the
left, push the Stone right to the collapsible section of Floor, and hang on the Mini-Ladder to
destroy the Floor. When the Stone falls on you,
climb the Ladder on the right, go left and drop
into the Pit, then eat through the Wall on the
left to the Monster.

Round 16: Break down the two lower right
sections of Wall, then climb the Ladder on the
right. Drop down the Pit on the left and knock
out the complementary sections of Wall—not
the one to your left, but the one to your right.
Knock the Stone right, get the lowest Monster.
Knock the Stone another space to the right—
so it's against the Ladder—then step left once
and let the Stone above you fall. Take care of
the last Monster in the middle, then eat away
the Wall on the far left so you're standing under the last Monster. Push the Stone right,
step right, let the Monster fall and cream it.

Round 17: Get rid of the Wall in the upper
right, but step to the right. Get the Monster on
top, then drop to the Ledge below, land to the
left of the Stone, and shove it over the side.

Push it next to the Monster's perch, then go back up the Ladder and shove the lower Stone over. Push it next to the one already below. Go back up the Ladder, across the top, down the side onto Stones, and get the Monster.

Round 18: Climb, use the Mini-Ladders to cross to the Stone on the left, push it onto the collapsible Floor and knock it down. You'll fall with it: walk right, eating away the Wall there, and climb the Ladder. Eliminate the Floor under that Stone, allowing it to fall beside the other. Climb the Ladder, drop down, and finish off the Monsters.

Round 19: Get on the Ladder, climb down a rung, eat away the Wall to the left and knock over the Stone. Push the lower one on top of it, and the rest is easy. On the right side: get rid of the Wall under the lowest Stone, go right, drop and come back up the Ladder, push the lowest Stone right, get on top of the Stones, eliminate the Wall under the topmost Stone, go right, down, left, and around again, push the top Stone over the right side, get on it and get the Monster.

Round 20: Use repeated trips up the Ladder to get rid of the Wall on the left. Cross over to the right, knock the Wall from under the top Stone, get the monster on top of it as well as the one to the right, then come back down. Chew away the Wall on the very bottom, freeing the Stone down there, and push it all the way to the right. Drop the Stone above on top of it and finish off the round.

Walking through the above rounds will give you an idea of what to expect in later rounds. However, there are still some toughies up ahead, for example:

Round 32: Stand Catboy at the edge of his Ledge, then have Catgirl push the Stone on top of his head. Place her between the Mini-Ladder and the Ledge on which Catboy is standing. Let him put down the Stone, push it onto and over the Mini-Ladder—so the Stone is on the right—place Catboy on the right side of the Stone and have Catgirl walk right over to the Monster.

Round 40: Climb the Ladder halfway and kick the lowest Stone on the left to the right. Knock over the Stone that was on top of it, get on top of it and destroy the Wall to your right. Step to the left, so you're on the left side of the Stone that falls. Knock them both off the Ledge to the right, head right and get rid of the two Monsters and the Wall between them, cut left and kill the Monster on the bottom, step *right* from under the Stone, then cross the Mini-Ladders and drop in on the two remaining Monsters. Use the Mini-Ladders to get to the pile of Stones to the left, eat away the Floor beyond it, climb the Ladder, knock over the three Stones on top, building a stack of three on the solid Wall below—but *don't* destroy the collapsible Floor up here—and kill the Monster on the right.

Whichever level you play, *don't* seize upon the obvious course of action: it's usually wrong.

Rating: B

The fact that there's no real danger for the feline pair will put a lot of players off. On the other hand, the fact that there *is* no violence, and the early rounds are very easy, make this game ideal for young kids.

COSMO TANK

Type: Seek-and-destroy

Object: Humankind has spread throughout the stars, but its progress is suddenly halted by insectlike beings also searching for new worlds to inhabit. At the controls of your Tiger Tank, you must visit five planets and beat back the aliens.

Hero: The Tank can move in any direction, fire a Laser, and detonate Bombs. The latter destroy any life form on the screen, and also bring down certain barriers. Upon dying, certain foes give you power-ups, which must be claimed within five seconds or they vanish. If you position yourself on one of your Bases —such as the one beside you when you start the game—your life-force may be restored, or you may get vital information. At any point in the game, if your Shields are low and you don't want to give up your accumulated power by dying, hightail it to a recharge Base for repairs. Whichever foe was attacking when you rolled into a Base will be gone when you roll out. In the 3-D views (see *Strategy*), your Tank is equipped with Radar to help you keep track of enemies, and a Compass so you can chart your way through the maze—directions in the Compass sections will be given using north/south/east/west instead of up/down/left/right, as in other theaters of combat.

Villains: These vary from enemies that simply roll at you, to aliens that hop up and down or circle you and fire back, to others that don't show up on your Radar, to still others that appear and disappear unexpectedly. All are discussed below.

Points: This game rewards you with Experience points, which are registered for every kill.

Strategy: While traveling between worlds, you'll be playing on a vertically scrolling screen that is similar to *SolarStriker* and other space games. No real problems here: you just shoot what's in front of you and duck under whatever you miss so you can take a second shot. On the planets themselves, you will fight in overhead (2-D) views when you're on the planet surface, and from-the-cockpit (3-D) views in Caves or buildings.

Make your way through the worlds as follows:

Desa: Get to the Cave by heading up, going left when the path opens in that direction, traveling up, and then moving diagonally to the upper right. When you reach the Wall, detonate a Bomb to get through, then turn left. Head up after a few moments and you'll come to the Cave. If at any point you're attacked by a Spider, either you can stand your ground and keep up a steady stream of fire—in which case you'll take only one hit from each Spider —or else you can get in a few shots, move to one side when the Spider fires, then resume shooting. If you're near a Base where you can recharge, you might as well take the hits. Inside the Cave you can kill virtually any foe you meet by swinging your tank in the direction *opposite* that in which your opponent is moving. When the Radar shows the alien almost at twelve o'clock, fire—and keep on moving at top speed. Your Laser will hit, but your enemy's usually will not. You don't even have to look at the creature: just adjust your sight and keep your eye on the Radar. Four hits will do 'em in. To find the first sub-boss, head north until you enter a door and come face to face with a Robot. (Even if you have to turn away to fight an alien, head north when you're through). Blast it, then head south until you can enter a corridor that leads east—you'll recognize the turn by the different way the wall posts are arranged. Take it until there's a passage to the north, then follow it until you leave the Cave. You'll emerge from a Crater and face not only Spiders and superfast Scorpions, but Mines that rise from the ground periodically: hit them and you'll lose energy. Head up, then left, and enter the Cave —on the alert for guardian Hornets, which buzz around the vicinity. Travel north. En route, you'll fight an alien that separates into two parts which head in opposite directions. Fire relentlessly while it's still in one piece; if you don't destroy it then and it separates, take out the slower, lower part first by keeping up steady fire as you follow it along, then use the radar plan described earlier to defeat the flying segment. Resuming your northerly journey, you'll enter the sub-boss room. Fight the creature, then check out the Map which looks like an H with a tail: head south, west, and south for the clear square in the tail section. (Note: each half arm of the H is three taps long on the pad.) Enter the room there to battle another sub-boss . . . a third Robot. (If you reach the Crab room now, you went too far! Go back to the Map room and start again.) When you win here, go to the lower left corner of the H to do battle with the Crab boss. You won't be able to take too many hits from this cosmic crustacean— three, to be exact—so notice which way it's scuttling and stay slightly ahead of it to that side, shooting it on the far right or left and shifting when the creature does. Notice, too, that before it switches from firing to the other side—or continues a new barrage on the same side—it ceases shooting for a moment: let that be your cue to be *ready* to shift your own attack if necessary! When you shift, *don't* cut across its line of fire or you'll be hit. Rather, swing all the way around and come at it from the other side. Make sure your Laser is amply charged —at least to two—before beginning your assault. If it's not, go out and kick some alien can until you've got the power you need. Upon defeating the monster, *don't* go to another planet. Choose this one again, reenter the Cave, and travel in a northerly direction. As you do, you'll automatically gather a ton of power-ups! *Then* you're ready to fly to further adventures. When you leave—via the Crater, *not* through the Cave door—head up and left for news about the Shield Unit (pssst: it's on Gadam!), the Hover Unit (on Monoa), and the Pulse Unit (on Aquel). Head to the upper right and you'll find another Base: this is your launch pad to other worlds! Here's how to conquer each:

Monoa: Head to the upper right, blast the Wall, continue up, destroy the next Wall, and keep going up. Enter the Base to the left for the Hover Unit, continue up and enter the Cave. You'll fight walking Eyeballs in here: they're only vulnerable when their lids are open, so avoid their fire until then. Stay on a course to the north until you emerge from the Cave via a Crater. Head up through the two Walls, stop at the Base to recharge, and roll to the left and up to enter the next Cave. Travel east and then north, prepared to battle a flying creature that continually changes altitude. Fight this one by flying along with it, constantly adjusting your laser-sight as needed. At the end of the northern passage is a sub-boss; make sure you're powered-up or you won't win here. You'll get a Map: head to the upper right corner, where you'll tackle a wormlike boss which constantly rises from the sand and then slithers back down. Needless to say, shoot only when it's exposed . . . and don't attack unless you've got at least two—preferably more—on your Laser meter.

Aquel: Go up, stop at the Base, and hover right, edging up slightly. Enter the Base on the island for information. Continue north and you'll reach the Pulse Unit Factory. There, you'll have to fight a boss whose Claws detach and come whirling at you. Stay to the side, avoiding the Claws, until the alien is at the top of the screen—in one piece!—then blast it. Head left to a Base, then go back down and to the right. Enter the Crater and go south, east, then north. Kill the Robot sub-boss and get the Capsule: there's a helpful ally inside! Once again travel south, east, then north to the next door. Destroy this Robot, head south, and exit. Journey up and left to the next Base, then continue in the same direction to a Cave. Enter and go north then east to reach the Robot here. When it's destroyed, you'll get a Map. This one resembles a T with two crossbars: the boss is located in the top crossbar on the right.

Gadam: Trek up and left to the Base, taking care of the Spiders before you enter—kill one fast (in the center, since they're closer) so you have a space under which you can duck while plugging the others. Chat with the woman there, then go down *around* the Crater to another Base. Here's where you get your Shield Unit. Head north, past the two rows of black markings, and enter the edifice. Beat the boss by moving to the side when it descends, then getting under it and shooting away. Leave, drive south—past the black markings—turn right and enter the Base you'll find there. Turn south for an encounter with the next boss. When you beat it, exit and journey up, watching out for the sand-filled Craters here; they'll wreak havoc with your Tank if you pass over them! Recharge your energy at the next Base, then head right. Drop into the Crater: it's actually the entrance to a Cave. Head north to fight the Robot sub-boss, get the Map, then go south, west, and north—to the top of the left H-like shape on the Map—for a showdown with another Crablike boss. When you win and leave the Cave, it's time to fly to . . .

DN-1: Travel up, enter the Base, then drop in the Crater a bit above it. Not much doing here, so exit—north, then west. Head up, keeping an eye peeled for Mines, then stop at the Base. Continue up, enter the Crater, travel north then east, exit and continue north. The scenario is more or less what it's been before: check out the Bases, enter the underground labyrinth, and destroy the sub-bosses and boss. The leader here is an extremely powerful Robot with a pair of aides. These are located on either side; de-

stroy them first, then hit the Robot himself. You'll
have to swing from side to side to avoid his powerful
blasts, but you've been down *that* road before! Just
make sure you don't hit the Robot's Cannon: do so
and his pesky assistants will reappear! Defeating
the Robot will win you the Sensor Unit. It'll also
earn you the right to go to a planet hitherto unseen
on your world-screen: Gidoro, the alien base.

Gidoro: You'll be battling familiar faces from the
past here, so while the action is thick, very little
will come as a surprise. Make your way up, enter
the structure and drop into the Porthole. Head
west, north, east, then turn south where the roads
meet. Take this path to the door to fight the sub-
boss. Return to where the roads crossed and go east.
When you're out of the building, turn right; drop
into the second Porthole. Destroy the alien *and* the
Bomb it's carrying, then go north, east, north at the
crossroads, and enter the portal for another sub-
boss showdown. Travel east, south, and east for a
third battle. When you've defeated this alien, it's
time to get back to the surface by heading west,
north, and east at the crossroads. Roll up, checking
out the structures you find—the second will spruce
up your Shields—then hop into the porthole you encounter. Head north and battle the sub-boss Robot
and get a Map. Your destinations, in turn, are the
second downward-pointing corridor from the right,
and then the rightmost corridor. Win here and
you'll face the supreme alien boss. If you thought
any of the previous extraterrestrials was tough,
wait'll you get a load of this spidery monstrosity!
The way to beat it is by disarming it (literally) on
the left and right, then turning your attention to its
domed head. When that's destroyed, fire away at its
Heart. It'll take a few continues to get the hang of it

—meaning you'll have to kill other aliens to power-up again before a rematch—but if you persevere, eventually you'll triumph.

Rating: C+

Many players think this is a great game because there are plenty of places to explore. On t'other hand, many find most of those places pretty much the same when you get right down to it. The graphics are spectacular, but once you learn your way through the impressive scenery, the game is just a notch above average.

DAEDALIAN OPUS

Type: Jigsaw puzzle

Object: The player must put the geometric shapes together so that they completely fill in an outline.

Hero: Your "heroes" are puzzle pieces that come in a variety of shapes. Many of these are discussed below and are self-explanatory. The higher the level, the more pieces there are.

Villains: None . . . except for puzzle walls, which refuse to bend and stretch. In other words, you can't wedge the pieces in any way other than the *correct* way!

Points: You play against a timer, and are rewarded with a password when you complete a level. The password's the same whether you take a half minute or a half hour to finish a puzzle.

Strategy: Taken level by level, the correct combinations for the early puzzles are:

1. T with its top along the left side, L on its back facing up with its bottom on the right; the rest is obvious. Password to the next level: KING.

2. Set the T upright in the center, with its crossbar along the top. Lay the L on its back, beneath it, its top butting the lower right side. The other two are obvious. Password: EASY.

3. You won't need the T here. Put the L on its back with the bottom facing left. Set the line flat on top of it, and place the fat L with its base against the right side, its back along the top. The rest is obvious. Password: NICE.

4. You won't use the "right angle." Put the line up against the left side and the T against it, the crossbar of the T flat against the midsection of the line. The fat L goes on the bottom, lying on its back with its base pointing right, and the L goes to its right, upside down. The rest is easy. Password: BORN.

5. No using the line this time. Put the U with its base against the left side and place the "right angle" facing left, the front of its base touching the U. Nestle the fat L between them. Put the crossbar of the T against the back of the "right angle," and the L on its back, its base against the right wall. The last piece is obvious. Password: FREE.

6. Skip the "right angle" on this one. Put the line against the wall to the right, the U next to it on the bottom, and the Z with its base along the line, its short top poking down into the U. Put the fat L up against the Z so that it forms a straight line with the left side of the U. Place

the T in the upper left corner with the cross-bar along the top, and the L standing upright beneath it, flush against the left wall. The placement of the last piece is clear. Password: STEP.

You get the hang of it. If you want to get to more difficult levels without waiting, the passwords are:

LIVE (8)	WILD (23)
CITY (9)	TIME (24)
MEGA (10)	SHOW (25)
SONG (11)	MOON (26)
LOVE (12)	EAST (27)
JUMP (13)	RAIN (28)
CORE (14)	LONG (29)
BEAT (15)	CLUB (30)
BURN (16)	TOWN (31)
SING (17)	WOOD (32)
TOUR (18)	BASS (33)
LOOK (19)	MIND (34)
SOUL (20)	STAR (35)
OPEN (21)	FINE (36)
BEST (22)	

Just for kicks, you'll want to input ZEAL as well!

Rating: B
A refreshing change from the shoot-'em-ups, though an element of pressure would have added to the play value: for example, the pieces scrambling themselves up after a certain time period. Still, you'll be challenged by this cartridge.

DR. MARIO

Type: *Tetris*-type game

Object: Dr. Mario has it easy: all *he* has to do is fling
Vitamins into a Medicine Bottle. Your task is some-
what tougher: you have to eliminate Viruses in the
Bottle by placing those Vitamins on or beside them.
The stage ends when all the Viruses have been
eliminated *or* if there's a Vitamin bottleneck in the
Bottleneck and Dr. Mario can't throw any more in!
Each stage has more Viruses than the one before it;
there are 20 stages of difficulty in all. (When you
beat Level 20, you see the viruses floating in what
looks like water with some kind of kelp growing
next to them. We can tell you how to win, but we
have *no* idea what the defeated germs are doing
lounging around at the bottom of the sea!)

Hero: The Viruses and Vitamin capsules come in
three different shades—black, white, and gray—and
each Vitamin is comprised of two parts, either the
same shade or different shades. The Viruses *or* previously fallen Vitamin sections can only be elimi-

nated when three other similarly-toned Vitamin
sections are dropped on top of, beneath, or beside
one that's already down. Four tones in a square
shape won't do it: they have to be horizontal or vertical stacks. If you interrupt the stack or row with
another color, you have to stack three matching
shades on or beside the *new* Vitamin section in order to eliminate it and regain access to your origi-
nal stack or row. You can twist the Vitamins so that
they fall flat or on end, and you can speed up their
descent and shift them from side to side as they
drop. Once they touch down, you have exactly *one
second* to shift it left or right as far as you want,
stand it upright, flip it over entirely—or any mix-
ture of those moves! When you stack or line up
a Virus and three matching tones, or four matching
Vitamin segments, all will vanish. If a solid-toned
Vitamin is placed on three other segments—thus
completing the row or stack with five segments in
all—all five will disappear. In the very neck of the
bottle, even if that topmost (fifth) segment of the
stack is a different color than the other four, it too
will disappear. A Vitamin can be left hanging: if
you put one side lengthwise on a vertical stack, only
that end needs to be supported. The other section
can hang over empty space, and other Vitamins can
be piled on *it*. These hanging segments and anything you've placed on them will drop if the sup-
porting stack is eliminated; if, in falling, that
section (or sections) completes a stack or row below,
it too will vanish. Note: in the following discussion,
"stack" means a vertical collection of segments,
while "row" refers to a horizontal collection.

Villains: The Viruses do nothing but sit there and
glow!

Points: You earn points for making Viruses disappear, not for placing Vitamins on the screen or getting rid of rows or stacks that consist solely of Vitamin segments.

Strategies: There are no specific strategies to apply on a screen-by-screen basis, since every screen is different and the sequence of the Vitamins you're offered changes from game to game. Here, then, are general tactics:

• The Vitamins always enter the Bottle facing the same way Dr. Mario is holding them. This is useful to know, just in case you have to slide one somewhere or flip one on end in a hurry.

• Because Vitamins can be shifted even after they've touched down, don't jump the gun on the Vitamin waiting in the "batter's box." By trying to move that one the instant it enters the Bottle, you may accidentally shift the previous Vitamin that hasn't quite settled in yet.

• Likewise, don't "overflip" a Vitamin. Many players tend to hold their finger on the button, lifting it when the Vitamin's been turned the way they want it. *Don't.* If you hold it one moment longer than necessary, the Vitamin will turn again . . . and not in any way that'll help you. This is especially deadly when, in early stages of later rounds, you're sliding Vitamins into the corner. If you meant to place a Vitamin down flat and it winds up on end, it may reach the top and block your access to the side of the screen.

• Always look at what's coming next: it'll influence what you do *now*. For example, if you see that your present piece will clear a row or stack and allow you to reach a Virus that the next Vitamin will remove —or bring closer to removal—take advantage of that.

• At the beginning in the higher levels, when you get solid-toned Vitamins, try to place them upright on the Viruses closest to the Bottleneck first, especially if there are two already in a stack or row. You'll want to get those out of the way to give yourself some elbow room.

• If you only need *one* more section to fill up a row of four, think about whether it's better to place the Vitamin on its side or on end: you might be able to start a new row or stack with the other section of the Vitamin. (Remember: when a stack vanishes, there are often Viruses underneath waiting to be built upon. Many players tend to overlook those, completing stacks by laying Viruses lengthwise.)

• Before adding a solid-tone Vitamin on three pre-existing row or stack segments—as mentioned earlier, causing all *five* portions to disappear—see if you can use that fifth piece on the side to start a new row or stack. There's no reason to waste a segment just because it's easier to get rid of the whole Vitamin! By the same token, eliminate that extra piece if, in falling, it'll block access to a pair or threesome of segments.

• If you have a choice of two or more rows or stacks in the Bottle that can be eliminated with a particular Vitamin, go for them in this order: highest with a Virus; highest without a Virus; lowest with a Virus. As mentioned above, it's important to keep the top of the Bottle clear so you can maneuver.

• If you have a Vitamin and no exposed matching tone on which to drop it, place it in a row without a Virus. Otherwise, you'll simply add to the length of time you need to get to the Virus—unless two solid Vitamins are coming in a row, in which case you can simply use the second to eliminate the first.

• Pursuant to the above, in the later stages it's imperative to create safe "corridors" in which you can deposit unwanted Vitamins. The last thing you want is to bury Viruses *deeper* as the Vitamins speed up. Having a corridor like that serves another purpose as well: you can use two-tone Vitamins more efficiently. Assume that the last corridor on the right is safe and the next stack to the left has a gray Virus on top. You can place a gray and white and then gray and black on the gray Virus without worrying how the different, unused Vitamin halves are stacking up in that far right corridor. Needless to say, it's even better to have safe corridors on either side of a Virus: that way, you can drop the unused half of two-tone Vitamins on matching segments, eliminating them rather than piling them up in a multitoned heap on one side. If you don't have a safe corridor or two in later stages, *never* stack two-tone Vitamins together if they have only one shade in common. In other words, if you have a gray and black Vitamin, followed by a gray and white one, don't match the grays up, leaving the other segments hanging off the sides. When you finally eliminate the gray, you'll have all those other segments to deal with—not an appealing prospect when Vitamins are raining like confetti! You can, however, stagger Vitamins this way in early stages:

when the center stack vanishes, it'll dump both sides, enabling you to finish them off. For instance, if you have four grays in the center, you'll have, at worst, two blacks and two whites on the sides . . . not a daunting prospect, especially if, in falling, they land on matching Vitamin segments of Viruses.

• Don't forget that you can attack a Virus from underneath. If there's an open passage to the bottom, you can slide a Vitamin *under* a previously placed Vitamin that may be blocking off a Virus. When doing this, you should watch for open sections where you can place a solid-toned Vitamin upright to finish a stack.

• In the later rounds, where Vitamins come faster and the Viruses are more plentiful, try to build rows rather than stacks. If you have no immediate need for a tone, put it *beside* one just like it—flat if it's a solid Vitamin—and if there's room—on end if it's two-tone. Spaces may open up on either side, suddenly making it possible for you to build a horizontal row of four or more.

• If there are isolated Viruses high on the screen and you can't pile Vitamins on top, don't leave the Virus there! More games are lost because of these hermit Viruses. Stack Vitamins one atop another to build up to them and eliminate them. This is easier to do when the Vitamins are coming at you slowly, in the early going. Obviously, when building up like this, make sure you stack *different* toned Vitamins on top of each other; if you stack the same tones on each other, they'll just keep vanishing when you've got four of them!

• One way of reaching those isolated Viruses is to build bridges—more accurately, staircases—across large gaps. Lay a Vitamin down flat, place another one flat on top of it, so that half of it's hanging over empty space, drop the next one on top of that Vitamin—also flat so that half of *it* is hanging over—and so on. The whole shebang will resemble a staircase and will enable you, for example, to drop a solid-toned Vitamin horizontally beside two others in an upper corner or to cut a section from the middle of a tall multitoned stack. When it comes time to eliminate the staircase, you can use each successively lower "step" to create rows with the Vitamin above it.

• In levels 19 and 20, if you can't open the stage by creating a stack or row of three or four, shove the Vitamin off to the side—obviously, on a matching tone—rather than drop it in the center. You can always get rid of "side clutter" later by creating rows or building up to the higher segments, as described above. But if you let isolated stacks of two—a Virus and one matching Vitamin part—collect in the middle, they'll pile up fast and the round will end before you know it!

• If you can slide a Vitamin into a stack vertically —that is, the Vitamin lying on its side—it's possible to take out up to eight segments of Vitamin and Virus at once by completing two preexisting sets of three. Unfortunately, the game won't let you take out more than that—meaning you can't use one piece to finish a stack above and below *and* a row to the side.

• Whenever possible, create several stacks, one for each of the identical two-tone Vitamins. It's easier to handle them when you know ahead of time where they're going—and, after you have just four of them, they'll disappear!

• Want to set up a row, but you don't have the support underneath? Consider the following. You may not be able to place a solid-tone Vitamin right next to the Virus or segment you want to take out. However, you might be able to put it horizontally on a support segment *two* places over. What you'll have, then, is the Virus, a gap, and the solid-tone Vitamin. All you need to do to create a row then is to drop enough Vitamins into the gap to fill it, enabling you reach the level of the three in the row you're building. When the right-toned segment comes along, slip it into the gap on end.

• It isn't as important in the early stages, but it's vital in the later stages: Vitamins that stand on end so that one segment is *completely* out the top of the Bottle only count as *one* segment. So don't plan on making that row of two disappear with a one-tone Vitamin: the game will read it as three segments, not four.

• In later stages, if you end up with a stack of three Vitamin segments and/or Viruses piled on the far left or right, with just one space between them and the top of the Bottle, it's often very difficult to slide a Vitamin on top of them. What to do? Using the same tones, build a stack of three right beside it. When a solid-tone Vitamin comes along, slide it over and eliminate both stacks. The addition of the extra stack gives you a place to land the solid-tone Vitamin before it falls, after which you can slide it into place.

• Suppose you have a stack of two matching segments being held up by a stack where there's three matching segments. For example, three grays in the center and two whites to the left. Suppose, further, there's a gap beneath the whites . . . below which there's another white. A solid white Vitamin comes down. *Don't* put it on the two whites. That will eliminate them needlessly. Use the solid white Vitamin somewhere else, wait until you can get rid of the stack of gray, and let the whites to its left *drop* on the white segment or Virus below. All you need, then, is one more white to get rid of the stack. Had you eliminated the two whites with the solid Vitamin, you'd have been left with the one white exposed after eliminating the gray stack . . . and nothing useful on top of it.

• Don't get smug when you've got the Viruses way down on Level 20. You'll be surprised how fast the unused Vitamins pile up! Players (this one included) have lost with just *one* Vitamin left on the screen, 'cause it got buried!

• Eventually, players who make it to the end of the later rounds will be faced with the following dilemma: there's a Vitamin on its way down which can be used to eliminate a row or stack containing a Virus, *or* can knock out a row or stack comprised solely of Vitamin parts—but which, when eliminated, will expose a Virus that is the only one of its color left on the screen. In this case, go for the latter: exposing a new Virus will give you one more useful place to put falling Vitamins.

• When trying to build rows, notice that you can drop a stack in order to shift a high segment in that stack to a point where it will add to or complete your row.

Rating: A
This is the game *Tetris* fans have been waiting for: a positively brilliant cartridge of that kind, but with all-new challenges and objectives. A must-have for your library!

DOUBLE DRAGON

Type: Martial arts quest

Object: You probably know this story by now: Billy and Jimmy Lee are twin, street-smart brothers and martial arts experts. Billy's a good guy, Jimmy a bad one known as the Shadow Boss. When Jimmy's hirelings abduct Billy's girlfriend Marian, family relations go by the wayside and our hero sets off to rescue her.

Hero: Billy can utilize various kicks, punches, and throws as described in the instructions. He can also pick up and use discarded weapons, also pictured in the instructions. Note: if a weapon thrown by an enemy strikes an enemy, the effect will be the same as if you threw it. Note too: a Jump Kick is more effective if you connect on the way down. Important: when you're Jump Kicking a foe using Jump Kick *and* pushing left or right on the pad, the second Jump Kick usually causes you to land right on top of your enemy. Getting up, he or she will be able to sock you one. Thus, as soon as you come down from

a second Jump Kick at the same foe, resort to plain
old A button Punches.

Villains: Though the bad guys have the same powers
as Billy, none has the same degree of stamina—with
the exception of Jimmy. Note: the description of the
order of attack of the villains below presupposes
that you make steady, relatively quick progress
through the game. If you tarry too long in one area,
you'll often be attacked where you are by additional
foes—usually of the same kind as the one(s) you're
fighting.

Points: Everytime you knock down a foe—even if he or
she isn't kayoed—you earn points. Everytime you
are hit, you don't lose points, but energy. You get a
one-up at 20,000 points.

Strategy: In general, if you find yourself in the thick of
too many foes, Jump Kick to get out of there. Not
only will that carry you away, but you may get
lucky and hit a foe! The game is divided into Mis-
sions. Here are the first three in detail:

Mission One: Take out the foe on the left with three
quick Jump Kicks, then turn to the crumb on the
right. Indeed, for the first four foes—who come in
groups of two—stick with the Jump Kick (the A and
B buttons) unless your foes get in too close in the
early going. If that happens, go with a Hair Pull
Kick—push the pad in your foe's direction, then hit
B. Pick up the Bat and use it to play a little T-ball
against the two Lindas who attack next, from the
doorway. (To make them emerge, go right, to the

second Drum from the left on the bottom, then cut
to the left and wait at the door on the right side,
whacking the pair as they come out. Don't stand
right against the wall, or the second one will avoid
your swings: stand toward the street a bit and you'll
get them both.) Jump Kick the next guy into oblivion—he comes from the left—with three fast hits,
then repeat with the next two bad dudes (hah!) who
attack one after another from the right. Three guys
come at you next. Get rid of the first attacker, on
the right—two Jump Kicks—then turn to face the
next two coming from the left, the foremost of
which is carrying an Oil Drum. Clobber him with a
Jump Kick; he'll throw the Drum, which will eliminate the guy on your right. Get the Drum and hurl
it at the thugs, then mix it up with your Jump Kick.
The next foes come right, left, then left, all of them
Lindas: Jump Kicks will put them away. Inside the
Warehouse—where any energy you lost will be restored—Jump Kick the enemy on the left into the
left wall (two Kicks) then Hair Pull him to defeat.
Jump Kick the attacker on the right until he's history. If you weren't able to pull this off, just Jump
Kick left and right until these two are finished. Continue to the right. When the thugs attack with the
Box, Jump Kick the guy holding it, grab the carton,
and do a little "Boxing." If you can, lead them to the
bottom of the screen and end the contest early by
knocking them off the Ledge. Enter the open door
and face the Abobo boss of this level. (Sorry . . .
you can't bring the Box in here.) Let him get in
close—just to the right of the last of the cabinets in
the background—and, with a Jump Kick, *superim-
pose* yourself over him, following him if he moves
downscreen and continuously pressing the pad right
so you're facing the brute's belly. Use repeated A
button Punches, keep him backed against the door,

and you'll have no problem winning. If he gets away
from you, Jump Kick over him again and get back
on his left side, punching right. Whatever you do,
stay in close: if he keeps you at arm's length, he'll
pulverize you. If you can't seem to pull that strategy
off, here's another: as he approaches, come toward
him at a diagonal down, then cut up, then down,
until you're right next to him. Go to Kicks or
Punches then. The zigzag is the best way to get in
close without him grabbing you. Either way, four
falls and he's out. The falls, incidentally, are not
always cumulative: if you only get him down three
times and you die, your next Billy *usually* has to
start all over again!

Mission Two: You're attacked, immediately, from
the right, but three Jump Kicks will take care of
him. Climb the Ladder—noting, overhead, the Conveyor Belt where you'll be in just a few moments—
use two Jump Kicks against the attacker who comes
from the right (that'll be enough to send him off the
Ledge), make sure you've walked past the door to
trigger it open, then hurry to the left and brace
yourself for an attack by two thugs. (If you stay to
the right of the door, you run the very real risk of
being knocked off the Ledge!) Two or three Jump
Kicks apiece will fell the felons. Climb the Ladder
and use three Jump Kicks to deep-six the Linda on
the Ledge—send the flunky onto the Conveyor Belt!
—then continue left to the Belt. Keep pressing left
on the pad as you cross; at the very end, Jump Kick
your way to the Ledge across the Pit and, without
stopping, Jump Kick to the next Conveyor Belt.
Make sure you keep pressing the pad left; otherwise, this Belt will carry you right and drop you
into the Pit. Ride the Belt to the Ladder and climb.
Two creeps will attack from the right: Jump Kick,

take a few steps to the left to put some distance between you and the other foe, Jump Kick again, go left again, Jump Kick, and so on until both are dead. A pair of Lindas will emerge from the doorway when you've passed it: hit the one with the Whip, pick it up, and make like Zorro, flogging them to insensibility. Get on the Elevator to the right and ride it all the way down. Head right at the bottom, Jump Kicking as soon as the first of two attackers appears to leap over the Dynamite he throws. Deck him with two Jump Kicks to the right, then Punch him out for good while the next guy is still climbing down the Staircase. When he arrives, you'll have polished off the first: three Jump Kicks to the left and he's kaput. Climb two Ladders, face a deadly duo, climb another Ladder, and face two more Lindas. If they crowd you and you can't resort to Jump Kicks, use the Hair Pull Kick—most effective here! Lead them to the Ledge and at least one will usually fall off. When they're dead, rush to the left side of the door, Elbow Punch the first guy who emerges, then Jump Kick the second. Like the first pair, lead them to the bottom of the screen and work at least one of them off the side. Hurry back to the left side of the door. When the Chintai boss emerges, you'll notice he has a nasty habit of not only beating you silly, but balling up and somersaulting out of range. So, go right to the door and, when he emerges, get in close like you did with the first boss . . . only this time, use the Hair Pull Kick on the blighter. Just throw him from side to side with it, staying up against the wall with the door, and he won't even get to ball up and somersault away! If you goof and he does, chase him, Kick him when he's curled up, then immediately get in closer and do the Hair Pull Kick when he straightens out again. If the fight gets away from the wall

and you still want to keep this short, work your way
to the forward edge, and he'll end up somersaulting
right off!

Mission Three: Two attackers are followed by a
third here, so you'll have to use Jump Kicks with
care: using one may cause you to land on another
foe, who'll punch your lights out. Now it's best to
rely mostly on in-close techniques; ordinary
Punches and Kicks work best because they're fast-
est. You'll need that freedom to turn and confront
the other attackers. The fourth thug drops from a
Tree: he can be Jump Kicked to the left until he
expires. In fact, you can tag him even as he's dropping! Two thugs follow from opposite sides: start
with a few Jump Kicks, after which you'll have to
rely on in-close fighting. Next up are Pilings which
you must cross using a Jump Kick. Go to the top of
the screen to make these crossings; otherwise, you'll
drown. You'll need one Jump Kick each to get over
the two gaps—don't loiter on the Pilings in the center, or you'll be attacked with no room to do battle;
be prepared to deal with a pair of Lindas on the
other side, one of them from the left. (Both are easily sent to dreamland with Jump Kicks—or you can
hold your ground and let the one behind you fall in
the drink, which she invariably does. Just control
your own impulse to Jump Kick to the left: you may
take the fatal plunge yourself!) Another pair of
thugs follows, after which you'll fight a lummox carrying a Rock. You can leap the Rock after it's
thrown, if you wish—let it hit one of the guys to
your left—beat the man, pick up the boulder, march
onward and throw it at the fool who attacks you
from behind. You'll be quickly set-upon by a foe
from the right, left, right, and left with no break
between them: take each one out *completely,* using

Jump Kicks, before turning to the next foe. If your attention is divided, you're doomed. A dual attack from left and right follows—Jump Kick right, left, right, left as long as you can, then move in for the Hair Pull Kicks—after which one mug comes at you from the left. It's boss time then: this Abobo slug is just like the first, and should be dealt with using the zigzag technique. He appears on the right, so stay in the center: wait until he comes left, then get in close and bash him with Punches from the right. And how about leading this horse of a man to water? It works: go to the left, where the shore cuts toward the bottom of the screen, bash him with Punches close in, and he'll stumble backward . . . right into the water! When he's finished, continue right, Jump Kick downward to the dock and battle two more bosses—a pair of Chintais. The advantage you'll have here is that you can get a Knife from one of them. Stay to the left and always try to keep the two of them on one side: if you end up between them, you'll get pummeled. Hair Pull Kicks are again your most effective offense. Climb the cliff beyond, fight the loons who attack, and face your third Abobo. Use the same tactics as before to win, after which your depleted energy will be restored. Deck the dude with the Rock, pick it up and use it against the crowd that attacks, then watch out for falling Stalactites in the next phase. Either race ahead or take a step or two back and wait for them to drop. Jump Kick over the rolling Rock, race down the Staircase, put your back to the bottom step when the Rock tumbles your way, then cross the moving Ledges. Beat the guys on the other side *fast* because the floor's going to vanish, then make short work of the Abobo by leaping him and, from the right, Punching or Kicking him off the Ledge. If you've gotten this far, you've experienced just about all the game has to throw at you. Here are the highlights of what follows:

Mission Four: You'll have to fight two more Chintais at the doorway—after putting away a horde of Lindas; beat them and you'll get your energy back. You'll be able to get a Knife next—assuming it doesn't get you—and after a few run-of-the-mill fights you'll tangle with Abobo. Fortunately, you'll have acquired a Whip with which to whack him. Next up are the killer Blocks: they move out from the wall to trip you up. Hurry past the first group, then, at the second, watch the lower left Block. When it has come out twice, leap the Pit and rush on. A Dynamite-toting thug appears from the left; knock him down at once, get the explosive, and toss it at another enemy. You haven't far to go to the end now. When fighting to rescue Marian, you'll face your toughest foe yet: Willy. Get close using the zigzag technique described for Abobo in Mission One, always staying *behind* him. Otherwise, he'll machine gun you to eternity.

Rating: A
The Game Boy *Double Dragon* is a faithful re-creation of the NES hit. If you like relentless action, great sound effects, and terrific music, this one's for you. Others may find it tiresome.

FALL OF THE FOOT CLAN

Type: Seek-and-destroy as you walk along

Objective: Reporter April O'Neil has been abducted by the fiendish Shredder and his cruel Foot Clan. As the heroic Teenage Mutant Ninja Turtles, you must battle the Foot Clan and Shredder's many other minions to rescue her.

Hero: You can be one of four Turtles, each of which has his own special powers: Leonardo wields a Katana Blade, Michaelangelo carries Nunchucks, Donatello swings a Bo, and Raphael packs a Sai. All of the Turtles can leap and crouch; when crouched, they fling Throwing Stars. You automatically become another Turtle when your present Turtle expires. Turtles lose energy when they're hit by a foe or object—such as a rolling Boulder or Motorcycle, which can't be destroyed—and regain it when they uncover Pizza, either in Slices, Whole Pies, or Boxes. These appear when you defeat a foe. There are also bonus rounds in which the Turtles' master

Splinter invites them to play a game: if they win, energy is also returned to them.

Villains: These are discussed at length in the instruction booklet.

Points: The Turtles earn points for every foe they dispatch or Pizza they eat. These, too, are listed in the instructions.

Strategy: Here's the stage-by-stage lowdown:

Stage One: After the first Parking Meter, enemies start coming from behind. Deal with the ones in front of you first: since you're walking in that direction, you'll *get* to them first! You can crouch behind the Barrels and use Throwing Stars to strike foes beyond. Hit the second Barrel to access the first bonus round. Note: when the bonus round prompt says "bigger," it means the number you chose is bigger than the correct one . . . not that the correct number is bigger! You'll drop underground now, and will be attacked in the air as you leap the first break in the Walk. Be ready to hit back! A Boulder will roll at you as you climb the Staircase after your second leap. After the Bats, walk *under* the Pipe, right into the Wall, to enter another bonus stage. On the surface again you'll face the same foes, only more of them—along with the Motorcycles. You must clear these *completely* when you leap, or you'll lose energy. Afterward it's back into the Sewer, where you have to watch out for falling Blocks. These can be broken if you attack in time. When you fight Rocksteady, get in close and mix it up.

When you can, jump up and get behind him, so you can get in your blows without being hurt. Any power you lost will be restored when you're victorious.

Stage Two: Get through the rising and falling Columns by taking a step when it's up, ducking when it comes down, rising and taking a step when it goes up, crouching when it descends, etc. Ride the second down-Column as it descends, and hack at your enemy on the other side: if you simply leap over the Column, you'll land on him and it'll cost you energy. As you continue, you'll spend your time hitting left, right, left, right, since foes are thick on both sides. Also watch out for more falling Blocks here, and for another five rolling Boulders after them—the last one is on top of the Staircase. When you reach the top of the steps, leap up to jump through the ceiling. You'll climb more steps—watch out for the Boulder and, a moment later, an attack from behind—after which *drop* off of them rather than jump off: if you leap, you'll land in the midst of a group of enemies. When you reach the single Columns, you must jump from one to the other without touching the ground: each time you hit the hot Coals below, you lose energy. Take the jumps with a full push to the right on the controller: you'll need all the distance you can get. However, before beginning this trek, jump off the last batch of Columns and then push left and land *back on them:* this will bring on a foe *before* you start your crossing. Killing him now is easier than having to fight him from a precarious perch! Watch for the Pizza Box flying above the tallest of the Columns. After the first set of Columns comes another set, along with more of the same kind of foes you've been fighting. When it's Bebop time, the punk charges from the left.

Rather than try to face his charge now, jump, get behind him, and attack. He's particularly vulnerable in his Bebop-hind. Make sure you leap around him or crouch when he fires his beams at you!

Stage Three: Nothing out of the ordinary here as you leap from Truck to Truck. There are simply lots of enemies front and back. When you jump onto the Flatbed Truck, watch out for the Foot Soldier who rises from under the Cargo and throws it at you: jump it, then clobber the guy who threw it. Baxter Stockman awaits at the end of the convoy: he'll come at you from the right, so jump up and meet him with an attack of your own. He'll be spitting Fireballs at you, so get out of the way of each wave by moving left or right; take a mighty leap at him, whack him, and repeat as often as necessary. Four solid hits should take care of the winged wimp.

Stage Four: Stay on the floating Logs in the initial stages of the Waste Dump Ravine. Don't let yourself get scrolled against the left side of the screen or, more often than not, you'll end up in the water . . . and helplessly on top of a deadly Doughnut or Filet o' Filth. You'll have to walk underwater after the first set of Logs; no serious problems there. Make sure you leap up to meet the diving Foot Soldiers, since they're easier to defeat when they're diving than when they're chasing you. If you don't slay them in the air, come down *behind* them, and use your Throwing Stars or weapon to do them in. (When you jump, the Fish vanish as you hit the water! That's good news if you want to fight as little as possible . . . bad news if you want the points.) More Log-walking follows, with another polluted lake after that; the first Foot Soldier who attacks from underwater—*not* the diver from the left—will give you a Slice of Pizza. When you reach the cavern, the foes are the same—only there's more of them, along with Boulders (occasionally two at a time) and more falling Blocks. In this phase, take out foes left or right *as soon as they appear,* rather than waiting to attack the dudes on the left. After the second Boulder, turn to the left to face a Foot Soldier who'll attack swiftly from that side. Shredder is your enemy at the end of this round. Attack him from behind, but don't get complacent there: he has a nasty habit of disappearing and reappearing somewhere else, forcing you to get close and leap him again. His Sword makes a frontal assault all but suicidal.

Stage Five: To begin with, turn left and jump up: you'll enter a bonus round. Back in the real world, this level's a killer! You'll be sizzled from above by Lasers, and the Rodneys not only hurt you if they touch you, but they fire a Laser at you. The instant one of these guys shows up, leap up and hit it in the head. One shot'll do it. Otherwise, they have to be hit twice: once from the front before they fire, then struck from behind—they won't let you take two shots at the front: they'll zap you after the first. When you come to the first Lasers, hurry past them both the instant the first begins to sizzle. You'll be attacked here, so be ready to face a slew of foes. A Rodney will attack from the left, and there are more Lasers up ahead. When the Spine Stretchers arrive, leap them: they're just not worth fighting. You don't have any such luxury when Krang shows up. Stay to the left and, when he emerges from the right, hit him. He'll try to kick the shell out of you (or vice versa), then will jump and try to pounce on you. When he leaps, scurry beneath him, attack from the rear, and repeat as often as necessary.

Now, you know you can do level select in the game, but what you probably *didn't* know is that you can also do bonus level select! During the title screen, press the pad down while simultaneously pushing the A and B buttons. Still holding everything down, push select then start. The normal "configuration" screen will appear . . . but with an added "?". Choose that to go to the bonus rounds.

You can also power up at any point during the game by hitting pause, then pressing the pad up, up, down, down, left, right, left, right, B, A.

Rating: A
This is one of those something-for-every-age games. Small children will have fun with the first two levels, while experienced Game Boy players will be challenged by the next three levels. The graphics and music are excellent.

THE FINAL FANTASY LEGEND

Type: Role-playing quest

Object: In a time of magic, a bold quartet sets out to stop the Tower from sending Monsters into their realm, and to locate Paradise on the other side.

Hero: You can play a Human, Monster, or Mutant, each of which begins with a basic weapon and now money. You earn greater strength (Hit Points) as you win battles, the results of which are decided by the computer. (Note: when you're in a shop, be aware that you can *scroll* the items. Many players don't realize this, and end up selecting from just the list that's on the screen.) The more Hit Points you have, the stronger the weapons you can purchase. All characters have the ability to converse with people they meet.

Villains: Monsters such as Goblins, Zombies, and Lizards will seek to bar your way.

Points: There are none, per se: just the Hit Points described in *Hero*.

Strategy: The questions we've heard most frequently regarding this game are not how to win: that's relatively easy, believe it or not. The instruction booklet gives you an excellent overview of what needs to be done, along with some very helpful maps; all you need to do is build your Hit Points, arm yourself to the teeth, talk to just about everyone you meet, and the rest is like playing connect-the-dots: you go from place to place doing what must be done.

The questions players ask are these: What are the best characters to play and how the heck do we get started? Addressing these and other points . . .

To begin with, play Humans or Monsters; the Monsters are especially good in the later levels. What's important to remember about Monsters, of course, is that they need Meat to grow. In the early going, the only way to *get* the most Meat is by defeating the strongest evil Monsters. You'll find these—such as the Red Bull—by journeying to the southwestern regions of the first level. Mutants can be helpful in certain situations, but frankly, they're more trouble to keep fit and powerful than they're worth. For example, they get experience by striking the final blow in a battle . . . something that is *not* always convenient to arrange! Also, before you get under way, keep in mind that you're going to want to get the key acquisitions in this order: Armor, the Sword, and then the Shield. Make notes—and, of course, a map—of conversations you have with people you meet.

For the Humans on the team, boost their Hit Points to 200 and don't let them drop below that.

Also, buy Strength and Agility from the shops: those are enormously valuable to Humans!

Another general rule: don't overextend yourself. Because of the "save" feature built into the game, you may be tempted to go as far as you can as soon as you can. Don't. Go no farther than you should based on your abilities, or you'll be spread much too thin in the late going. For example, if you go to the Bandit Cave before you're properly armed with a powerful weapon such as the Axe or—slightly less desirable—a Long Sword, the Frog there is going to slaughter you. You can get the strongest weapons in this phase of play right in the Base Town where you started.

When you begin the game, don't even *think* of leaving town without putting your group together. Just go to the Inn—which is located right above you—head to the east, and you're in the Guild. Build your roster here. We've found that one Human male, one Human female, and a pair of Goblins works especially well. When that's done, exit the Inn, head in any direction, and you'll find yourself on a patch of land surrounded by Rivers. Leave the Island via the Bridge in the northeast—let's call it Bridge A because you'll need to remember it—and battle the evil Goblin. The Monster is usually easy to beat after it gets in one or two hits. Continue south and to the east until you come to a Town. Enter and, after checking it out, head to the east and then north through the Forest above the Castle. (You can explore the Castle now, if you'd like, just to familiarize yourself with it.) When you reach the Water, continue north until you come to a Stream with a Castle on the other side. You'll inevitably encounter a Monster here, which can be bested without much fuss. Cross the water and enter the Castle: turns out the King would love to have a word with you. Go upstairs and have a chat: the King will tell you about his missing love; it doesn't take much imagination to figure out where you're headed next. Journey south, battling any Monsters you meet—if you haven't lost too many Hit Points till now—and crossing four Streams below you. Then enter the Town. Trek north, ask around, and you'll find the King's beloved; she'll tell you why she fled, which will send you off on the next leg of your journey, to the Bandit Cave in the west. You'll have fought and beaten three or four Monsters by now—especially if you checked out every inch of the Forests on your way here—so it's a good idea to use some of those hard-earned Gold Pieces to purchase some weapons here. If you have enough Gold, you'll be able to purchase 200 Hit Points from a merchant. You can't make a better investment than that!

The Cave you seek is actually to the southwest; you'll get there quickly after crossing a few Streams. Once you enter, avoid having a talk with the first two figures you encounter, unless you're ready to battle a powerful Monster or two! Instead, take a stroll to the east and begin exploring the Cave. The route to the Bandit King is this: climb the Staircase you find, head southwest, and, after battling a Skeleton, enter the doorway in the west. You'll locate the Bandit King at the end of a long corridor. Not surprisingly, he'll reply "No Way!" to your order that he stay away from the real King's girlfriend; naturally, you aren't going to stand for that. He's going to summon a powerful Frog to champion his cause, so don't come here unless you're armed to the gills as described above! In the event that something unfortunate happens to one or more members of your party here, you can return to the last Town to visit a House of Life. It's located at the end of a Pier just north of the Bridge by which you exited the Town. After you defeat the Bandit Chief, his reluctant girlfriend is going to be *very* happy. Likewise, her pal the real King. Return to his Castle for your reward . . . and word on how to continue with your quest! Hint: there's another Castle on this level. Where you left the Base Town and crossed Bridge A, head south and then turn west when the River does. Walk south to the line of Trees, journey over them to the west, cut south when they do, cross the Bridge and follow the River east, south, east, south, east until you come to a Bridge to the north. Cross it and continue north to the Castle. You may encounter a Wererat in here, and it's a killer. (Make certain you've saved the game before you enter!) Surviving the Wererat, you'll make your way along the staircases and come face to face with Karateka, who'll make the previous fight seem like a day at Disneyland! You'll also find that several of the Monsters attack in tag-team pairs here, so make *sure* those Hit Points are way up there!

You can see by now that this isn't going to be a quick or easy game! As long as you take the time to keep your strength up, all you need to make it through is patience and common sense!

Rating: A
While not *quite* as complex as comparable adventures for the NES—notably *The Legend of Zelda* and *The Adventure of Link—The Final Fantasy Legend* is a masterful achievement for the Game Boy unit, and a superlative game of this kind. Role playing buffs will eat it up like they were Monsters faced with Meat!

FIST OF THE NORTH STAR

Type: Martial arts combat

Object: Various Lords each want to become the supreme ruler of a postnuclear war world. To this end, they agree to a round robin martial arts tournament to determine who is the most powerful . . . and thus most fit to rule.

Hero: You can play the part of any of 11 Lords. Each has his own powers, as described in the instructions.

Villains: Whoever you *don't* choose to be from that list of 11 is your enemy! Their powers remain the same, though the game tends to play very relentlessly against you.

Points: You lose energy when hurt, and gain Experience Points when you're victorious. The more Experience Points you earn, the more powerful you are at the start of your next battle.

Strategy: Two general tips: once you decide which character you're going to play, take *another* character, play against the one you're *going* to be, and watch how the computer handles him. Another good idea is to practice by simply *avoiding* an enemy's attack. Play pure defense to build up those skills.

Assuming you take the part of Kenshiro, here's how to tackle each lord in turn:

Heart: Go to the far left at once, crouch facing Heart, and hit the A button over and over, rapidly, until Heart gives out.

Shin: Get him with Aura Waves. Crouch, build up your power, and fire *an instant before you rise.* Instead of jumping or ducking, he'll just stand there. Make sure you jump his Vacuum Drain blasts, though: they take away any built-up A button power when they hit!

Jagi: Use an all-out Kick attack on Jagi: while his A button meter fills up, rush in and, standing as close as possible, Kick him until he retreats. Rush him again and repeat. When he jumps, turn and pursue him in that direction. The only time you have to break off the attack is when his A button meter fills and he's ready to Needle you! Even then, as you leap his repeated shots, jump so that you keep moving toward him.

Uygur: The guy's a Whipmaster, and is also fond of ramming you. You can Kick him while standing—your leg will reach under his outstretched arm—though you run the risk of trading blow for blow as he whips you. Since this Lord doesn't leap or duck, it's better—if not quite so daring—to Aura Wave him. Back away from him, zap him, recharge, zap him again, leap him, face him and repeat. You can recharge even as you leap and back away, which is a distinct asset! (Note: if you get next to him when he's not whipping, you can push him back—another way to buy yourself time to recharge your Aura Wave!)

Souther: This clown has a Vacuum Drain that radiates outward in three parts. That means you can't get in close if you plan to fight with your Aura Wave: if you try to leap or duck, you'll still get hit. And it'll take some seriously precise jumping to hop so that you're between the middle and top beams. Yet Souther is easy to beat. Just keep the pad pressed in whatever direction he is—he tends to hop over you from time to time—and, without crouching, *stay in close, Kicking.* He'll fall without getting off a single Vacuum Drain.

Raoh: You're going to have to beat him with Aura Waves . . . even though his are three-parters that fly at you in parallel paths. Jump them (easy enough) while you reload, crouch, fire before he's about to make his next shot—he usually won't duck your Waves then—and leap up immediately after you fire (to keep from being struck by his next Wave). Raoh doesn't even have to be on the screen for you to beat him this way: just watch his meter!

Falco: His Aura Waves come in two parallel blasts: fight him exactly as you did Raoh, when his Wave meter is two-thirds full. Handle Han the same way.

Hyou: Don't let the Boulders here throw you. Unless you want to climb on them, get in close and do some under-the-chin Kicking, play this round the same as above. The only difference is that you should wait until Hyou's Wave meter is just over half-full, then do your crouch, fire, and leap routine.

Kaiho: This guy's a tough cracker . . . but you can beat him as you did Hyou, using Aura Waves. Just wait until *his* meter is nearly three-quarters full before doing the now-familiar number on him.

Beat him, and you get to see the typo "Congratulation!" instead of "Congratulations!" which comes just before the credit scroll . . . where the "composer" is listed as "compose."

Rating: D+

Once you've won the game, it's entertaining, but hardly thrilling, to go back and find different ways of winning. Lack of diversity from one character to the next also hampers enjoyment of the game. And if this is a postholocaust world, why not *use* some of those elements—mutants or fallout or whatever—to give the game a sense of place?

FLIPULL

Type: Ricochet puzzle

Object: There's a stack of Blocks with one of four different designs on them. Using Blocks with those designs, you must throw your Block at the stack — directly or through ricochet—and hit a Block with a similar design. Each time a matching Block—or Blocks, if they're in a row—is hit, it disappears. Reduce the stack to the level specified on the screen, and you're bumped up to the next.

Hero: The player has the ability to climb a Ladder and throw Blocks.

Villains: The clock . . . and Blocks of different designs that are in your way.

Points: You earn points for each Block you eliminate, padded by the amount of time left on the Clock when you finish.

Strategy: Level-by-level specifics won't really help with this game. Thus, here are general tips:

• Whichever Block you hit, the next one you'll get is the one to the left of it . . . even if there's an empty space between them. If there isn't a Block to the left, then the Block below it will hop out. Clearly, you should be aware of which Blocks are where when you throw: you don't want to hand yourself a Block that has no accessible counterpart! If that *does happen,* if you can't use a Block, the game will give you an S, thus allowing you to use it on that row. However, like Aladdin's Lamp, you only get the S privilege three times, after which you get diddly and the game ends.

• Use the S Block you get at the beginning of the game to take out the longest row you can find. It's a wild card and will work on anything. When an S Block appears in the stack, play as if it weren't there: the Block you throw will go right through it.

• Since you always know what Block is coming next, be ready to move yourself into position. That will save several seconds in each stage.

• If there are no accessible rows to gun for, go after a Block that will give you a Block like one near it. In other words, if you have a Square Block and, exposed on the stack is a Square with a Taito Block to its left and above it, go for that one. You'll get the Taito Block from behind and can throw it at the one above. The less you have to move about the screen, the more time you save.

• Remember that Blocks you throw will finish off a row even if the next Block is at an angle. It'll go two across and then down, if that's the way similar Blocks are arranged. In fact, the Block you throw will travel down even if there are several empty spaces between the last Block in the horizontal row and the Block down below.

• If there's only one Block in a row, that's the one you'll get next turn.

• When a Block is removed, the Blocks on top of it are going to drop down one. That may expose a useful Block behind it . . . something to look for when planning your next move.

• You only get three continues. If you squander them early, you might as well start the game over again.

Rating: C+

There's no doubt that this game will make you think . . . but despite its ingenuity and the obstacles it throws at you, there isn't much versatility in the gameplay, nor does the player have very many options. You pick your target and throw—that's it!

GARGOYLE'S QUEST

Type: Fantasy quest

Object: The Ghoul Realm has been invaded by the Destroyers, an evil race of aliens. Firebrand, a denizen of the Realm, is the heroic Gargoyle who flies forth to locate the Great Fire—the only force capable of stopping the invaders.

Hero: Firebrand can fly—hover, really—spit Fireballs, and climb Walls. He can collect various power-ups as he flies, which are used to earn extra lives.

Villains: There are a slew of them, many of which are pictured in the instruction booklet.

Points: There are no points.

Strategy: Begin your journey by reaching the Tree and flying up to the *left* to claim a Vial—you can reach

it if you get on top of the tree, standing as far over
the left edge as possible, then pressing A and left on
the pad to get the height, then again to get the distance. Drop down the right side of the Tree—there's
nothing to the top right—and wait on the ledge for
the Bone Snapper to jump high enough for you to
shoot it . . . or cling to the Ledge and shoot it. (Be
careful: it might hit you!) Plug the Bone Snapper
across the way, then climb up the Walls until you're
holding onto the Ledge right below the Flame Head
and Ghost. Jump to the left and hover, face right,
and blast your two foes—the Flame Head takes two
shots to kill. Fly to the upper left for the Vial, then
continue to the right, kill the Bone Snapper, and
climb the Walls again. Hop up to the Ledge on the
right, ascend the Tree, kill the Flame Head, and get
on the very top of the Tree. Fly from that point to
the left to get the Heart. Return to the Tree and
cling to the top right side: from there, shoot the
Flame Head on the right. Hop onto its Ledge and,
immediately upon landing, shoot to the right to destroy the Malgor that will attack. Keep firing to the
right to Hive Creature beyond. When the latter
beast dies, fly to its Wall, drop to the left—landing
between the rows of Claw Plants—and shoot the
Ghosts on the right. Walk to the right, continually
firing, and get the next Hive Creature. When you
reach the Bridge, fly to the plank right above the
Vial. The Bridge will collapse and, collecting the
Vial as you fall, drop to the right, onto the Ledge
there. Keep up a steady fire, and try to kill the Bone
Snappers as you drop. Kill them as you proceed to
the right, then climb the Wall on the right, then the
one on the left, then go left. At the top of the Tree
fly to the upper left and get the Vial there. Return
to the top of the Tree and jump over to the right,
landing on the Ledge with the Claw Plants. Con-

tinue right, through the Ghost tunnel, and get the Vial near the end. Drop down the passageway and grab hold of the Wall on the left: there's a Heart at the bottom. When you've grabbed it, fly over the Claw Plants to the right. Cross the Pond and, at the Wall, be prepared to fight the giant Skeleton Fish. Retreat to the Ledge in the upper left when the monster charges, but keep shooting it: when it dies, the Pond below it will dry up and you'll be able to continue.

That'll get you started on this very *long* quest. It's important to master the basic skills or you won't get far. However, if you're having trouble—or even if you're not, and are impatient to get ahead—here are some increasingly more powerful passwords:

ULY7-66LC
HST8-7HRO
BMV5-RRBS
T5YO-UZEY
NTAN-RRX7

Check that last one out! Talk to the people you find here, make an expensive purchase, then go out and enter the portals that lead to a slew of Boss monsters!

9CJA-5LHB

That'll take you nearly to the end of the game as well, but without as much power. And if you want one that'll take you even farther—to the last town with a full load of supplies, weapons, and lives, the code is:

NPAN-RRXY

Rating: A

It's tough getting started on this one, learning the nuances of how to work your Gargoyle. However, once you master the skills, the game is truly a great adventure in the tradition of *The Legend of Zelda*.

GODZILLA

Type: Maze game

Object: Minilla—Minya in the movies—has been abducted by evil monsters and hidden in the vast maze Matrix. Godzilla, his father, must get through all 64 Monster-infested sections of the labyrinth to rescue his pint-sized heir.

Hero: Godzilla's greatest power is his ability to breathe Fire—even though they look like puffs of smoke in the game. He can also climb Ladders and Vines, and move the giant Rocks that block his way, dropping them on enemies, using them to block passages, or moving them for use as stepping-stones. In any case, all the Rocks in a given section must be destroyed before Godzilla can leave. Power-ups are a Sandglass, which paralyzes enemies; a Heart, which boosts Godzilla's energy; and Thunder, which slays every foe on the screen. Godzilla can only exit a section when he steps on an Arrow; these appear when he's cleared the screen of Rocks. Often there are more than one Arrow, so check the Entire Plan screen—or the advice below—before making a move.

Villains: These are listed in the instruction booklet. Hedrah—Hedorah in the films—is perhaps better known by his film epithet, "The Smog Monster." Incidentally, though he can't be destroyed, he *can* be pushed back by Rocks or Godzilla's Fire. Note, too, that Rodan has a flying pattern: the Monster moves in a wavelike pattern, flying up and down. Plan your shots at the leathery reptile accordingly! Monsters standing on top of Rocks will be destroyed when the Rocks are moved. Note: even when you've captured Thunder and cleared the screen of Monsters, they'll return via one of the doorways within seconds!

Points: You build your score by slaying monsters or destroying Rocks. You get no points for using Thunder to kill Monsters.

Strategy: Get on the bottom, under the Wall, and stay there until the first three Monsters have been destroyed. Stay about halfway up the second Vine to await the next Monster, from the left. When you reach the Rock on top, knock it down. When it lands, go to the right of it, kill the Rodan that attacks, and destroy the Rock. You'll get an Hourglass. Push the next Rock down when all the Monsters are to the left of the Wall. Go down to the right of the Rock and slowly push it to the left, destroying all Monsters by so doing. When they're all dead, destroy the Rock. Follow the arrow down. Here, you've got to climb from level to level. Hurry past the Doorway before Hedrah emerges . . . otherwise you'll take a hit or two getting past ole Smoggy. Destroy the Rock in the upper right, collect the Thunder, and descend again. You'll fight Rodans throughout and, when you reach the level just above the bottom, wait until Hedrah is headed left before climbing to the bottom level. Otherwise you'll have to push the beast all the way to the left to reach the Arrow, increasing your chances of being it. Follow the Arrow down. In the new section, smash the Rock on the bottom, then don't break *any* other Rocks . . . yet. Climb the Vines on the left, cross the first two Rocks, and stand on the second: knock over the third Rock from the right. When it falls, it'll destroy the Wall that keeps you from the left half of the section. Turn and knock down both Rocks on the right. Descend via the left Vine and destroy the three Rocks on the bottom in this order: right—by pushing it right, against the Stone—middle, then left. (If you push the one on the right to the left, it may fall on you as you smash the middle one.) Climb the Vine on the right, knock down the second Rock from the left, get back onto the Vine and knock down the remaining Rock, then destroy the one on the right by pushing it right. Smash the last Rock by shoving it left, then take the Arrow on the left—the one on the right will take you back to the previous room. Get to the Arrow by climbing the Vine, walking right, and dropping onto it.

In the next section you'll have to knock down the four Rocks as you go, but do it standing *two* steps to the left of each one: otherwise, the Rock on top will fall on you. Move the Rocks when there are Monsters to the right or below them, so you kill the beasts as you proceed. Just don't stand below the Door on top until a monster has emerged, or else you'll get nailed! On this level you must sweep back

and forth, dropping the Rocks without dropping
down yourself before a level is cleared; otherwise,
you won't be able to get back up and finish all the
Rocks off! Also, don't destroy any Rocks yet or you'll
be stranded. When the lower left corner comes into
view, wait until Hedrah is on the way down the
Vine before you press on. Even better: drop one of
the Rocks on him when he's on the *bottom* level, not
the second. (Another *one* will attack in a few seconds, but you can knock the Rock from under his
feet and kill him too! Another *two* will attack if you
kill Hedrah on the level just above the bottom. That
situation—three Hedrahs in one level—is really difficult to overcome.) Fail at the first killing of
Hedrah, and he'll pursue you. If that happens, when
you reach the bottom on the right side, turn quickly
and keep knocking him back to get to the Rocks;
other Monsters will attack simultaneously, so you'll
have to destroy them and the Rocks and keep
Hedrah back in the same breath (literally). It can be
done, but it's tough. The good thing about this tack,
though, is that if you *can* pull it off, there's Thunder
in a Boulder down here to help you. Important to
note: don't shift any Rock in this section until the
one in front of it has fallen out of the way. If the two
connect, the second one will be obliterated, thus
stranding you. Go to the Arrow-up in the middle of
the bottom level. The next section's a cinch: you'll
be walking down a Staircase pushing Rocks. Just
push one Rock over and beyond the one below it—in
other words, two pushes—destroy the latter, then
push the former twice again (over and beyond the
next). Don't *ever* stack the Rocks one atop the other
and try to destroy the one on the bottom. Obviously,
you'll be crushed! Return to the top of the Staircase
at the end and take the Arrow pointing up. This
section requires some running. Push the top Rock

all the way to the right, smashing it and the one to
the right. Go back to the Ladder in the middle,
climb down, head right, and destroy the Rock there.
Repeat and destroy the Rock below it. That clears
the right side. Go back up the center Ladder, destroy the top Rock by pushing it left, go down and
destroy the bottom Rock by pushing it Right, then
take out the middle one by pushing it left—the bottom Rock will simply fall onto the Spikes if you
push it left. Climb up the center Ladder and head
right on the level above to get to the Arrow. Next
section's a piece of cake: smash the two Rocks on
the bottom, then climb the Vine on either side, drop
onto the Rocks stacked above you, obliterate the
center one, knock the other two off the Ledge, then
pulverize them. You'll get an Hourglass from the
Rock on the right. Climb the Vine again and drop to
the Arrow on the left.

Play "leapfrog" in this section, pushing one Rock
down over the other on one side, then repeating on
the other. When you're done, get on the top Stone in
the center and press down on the control pad. Drop
down to whichever side Hedrah's *not* on. Stand just
close enough to spit Fire at the Rocks and break
them all—including the Block one of them becomes
—then exit to the right. The next section's pretty
obvious: you've got to push all the Rocks to the side.
Start by shoving the one beside you to the left,
crushing the oncoming Monsters, then to the right.
Maneuver around the remaining Rocks to push
them right as well. At the conclusion, go to the top
Arrow on the right. The new section, too, is self-
evident: push the right column of Rocks to the right,
quickly—so you can step to the right, turn, and
blast Rodan—and push down the single Rock beyond, then do the same to the column on the left. Go
left, dropping to the bottom of the screen, smash the

Rock on the left, then work your way to the right. The Rock that landed in the far right corner will give you a Sandglass: when you grab it, you'll also exit the screen. Once there, face right, bash the first two Monsters that emerge—though, obviously, not Hedrah—then hurry to the left, smash the Rock in the top left, climb up the Vine it was on (pausing to blast the Monster dropping to your right), fire at the Rock on the right—after killing a few Monsters about to descend from above—drop and climb the Vine *that* Rock was on, and so on. Always take the time to shoot Monsters across from you, since you can't blast 'em while you're climbing, and they have a way of accumulating. All you have to worry about is that you stay a Vine ahead of Hedrah. The Sandglass in the fifth Vine from the left will help you get through the section. If you ever get stuck at the bottom of a Vine with Hedrah bearing down on you, just blow a few puffs of Fire to push him back, then climb. Exit via the Arrow on the right. As you do so, keep your finger on the left side of the contol pad: the instant the next section starts, you've got to *race* to the left and stand under the highest ledge. Otherwise, you'll be pounded into Godzilla-burger. Burn up all the Rocks to the right, climb the Vine, drop to the top Rock on the left, knock off the one on the right, spit at the one on the left, and the rest is obvious. Walk to the right side and take the Arrow pointing up. Next section: climb up the left Vine, down the right side of the Wall, up the next Vine, across the top, down the Vine, and knock off the first two Rocks. Wait until the Monsters (including Hedrah) come from the right, then bury them. Push the last Rock to the right, get the Sandglass, climb the Vine and exit.

On the next level you'll be able to knock Hedrah onto the Spikes below . . . a real asset! Another asset is the Rock on the top right, which has Thunder! This level, and the rest, are increasingly complicated, but you've got the drift of the game by now. The passwords to bring you to the different levels we've discussed thus far are:

GL6T	C47?
1XPK	71CL
39TN	JHJ/
L&=7	SC/W
T8CJ	?7QG
?=5Q	

Codes to take you farther include:

8W2H
C?#2
=M3K
Q41M
LC/W
MXRT

Also, WT7Q (The one on the upper left must go *under* the weak spot in the midsection on the right; you have to build a diagonal Rock bridge to the top-middle Rock and push that *over* the Wall onto the weak spot.)

GG1C (This one'll make you nuts: you've got to push the one on the right to the right *at once*, then dart left to avoid the one dropping at you. Push the fallen one to the right to form a ramp.)

T94/ (You've got to act fast once again: immediately breathe Fire on the Rock to the right, then hustle left to avoid the falling Rock. Use the Rocks in the middle to get to the Rock in the upper left and push it over the side.)

8QH= (Use the Rocks on the right to break the Stones. There's Thunder and a Sandglass here.)

B#QG
GH4/ (Knock down the Rock to your left, climb down and move it two to the left, climb back up and hit the Rock on the right, then hang from the bottom of the Vine to the right of the starting Block to hit the Rock atop the rightmost Vine. Use the Rocks you knocked down as stepping-stones between the Vines in the middle and on the left. Exit via the top Arrow.)

?KGQ
9T4M (Don't bust anything, yet: go to the left, come under the section and up the right, then mount your assault on the Rocks. You've got to break up the Blocks in the middle and build a Wall four Rocks high to get to the Rock on the far left. Take the top Arrow.)

HB2/ (Go left, down, up the right Vine, and push the Rock to the ground. Shove it right, using it to gain access to the Rocks and Vine on the right. This is the last Rock you'll destroy.)

=65= (You've got to knock down the Rocks on the left so they raze all three Block Walls. Start by pushing the second from the bottom to the right, then the uppermost right Rock to the right. You're going to be building two stacks—you'll end up with one Rock on the left pile and four on the right—and push a Rock from the top of the stack of four to destroy the lowest Wall. Push the two on the upper left last, both onto the rightmost of the two stacks. You'll notice you still haven't touched the lowest Rock: you'll need that last Rock . . . the one sitting just to the upper right of the low Wall you knocked down!)

Rating: A—

Unique and destined to give you hours of mental exercise. The music is inappropriate and uninspired, though . . . hence, the minus.

HEAVYWEIGHT
CHAMPIONSHIP
BOXING

Type: Ringside action

Object: Laced up and ready to rumble, you climb into the ring and fight successively tougher opponents. The view is from overhead when the fighters approach one another. When they're in close, though, you're glaring straight through your Boxer's transparent head into the snarling kisser of your opponent!

Hero: Your pugilist can throw five different punches with each fist, and can also defend himself from matching blows. When a foe goes down, or when he gets in a clinch with his adversary, your fighter can regain some lost Stamina by repeatedly jabbing the A button. You get one rematch against each adversary; lose a second time against the same opponent, and the game ends.

Villains: Your adversaries are pictured in the instruction booklet; specific strengths and weaknesses are discussed in *Strategy*.

Points: Unseen Judges award you points for the effectiveness of your attack each round. As you battle, a clock counts down the time remaining in each round.

Strategy: Keep your foe occupied with one fist while the other builds up power, and note what punches you throw most frequently during a round. If you keep your opponent to sevens and sixes on the Judges' cards, you're doing something right! When you knock a foe down, don't forget to tap your A button repeatedly: your power will build while you stand there. Finally, you'll do best against most adversaries if you cannibalize ability from Speed and drop it into Punch Power and Stamina. (Some players prefer doing the opposite: building up their Speed, ducking adversaries' blows, and letting their foes get tuckered out. That works, but it takes longer . . . and frankly, folks, that isn't boxing. It's *avoiding* boxing! Besides, the Judges usually give a round to the aggressor, not the defensive player. The one exception to this is when you fight the Champ: you'll be using a little more defense than offense for most of the game.)

Here's what you need to know about each fighter:

Lightning Lou: If you get this guy caught in a Straight to the Head series from either side, you can land five or six blows before he'll put up his Gloves. When he does, wait for him to put them down, then resume clubbing him. He'll dance a bit and try to evade your hits as his Stamina wanes, but he'll usually go down in three.

Tokyo Thunder: A flurry of Body Blows work best against this guy. You can often get in eleven hits without Mr. Thunder raising a glove! He's actually the easiest of the boxers to beat and will almost always drop in two.

Johnny Jab: Use the same strategy as you did against Lightning Lou, with one difference. You can only land three or four blows before he raises his gloves, at which point he'll duck to the other side. When he does, tag him there with a series of Body Blows; you'll be able to hit him with two or three before he slides away. If you can sneak in some Uppercuts, he's particularly susceptible to those. Resume with the Straight to the Head shots and he's history in five. (The only reason he'll last *that* long is because, more than any of the other fighters, when his Stamina's low he desperately dances away from you. That makes him tough to hit. When he does this, keep him on the "punch" screen by hitting him repeatedly with Straight to the Head shots and Body Blows even when his gloves are up. *Don't* use Hooks on him in these latter rounds: they enable him to slide off the opposite side of the screen.)

Lefty O'Hook: You can turn this guy to cauliflower salad by keeping him to the right side of the screen and repeatedly firing Right Hooks alternating with right Body Blows. Shift to your left hand only if the palooka slips to that side. By the end of the third round he may have slowed down enough so that you can put him away with a few Uppercuts. He won't make it to the fourth if you get behind a relentless attack.

Mike Mauler: He's hard-hitting and dodges constantly—not just down, but to the sides—so you're going to have to keep up a varied attack against the guy. First, you've got to get him into one of the corners to keep him from running. When you get him there, Uppercuts will sink him best.

The Champ: It's almost impossible to beat him on the Judges' cards, so you'll have to win with your fists . . . which is *far* easier said than done! He moves around more than any of the other fighters, and it's super-tough to get him into a corner. Chase him, and hit him with the Straight to the Head shots or Hooks. Stay away from the Body Blows: they aren't going to damage this dude much. Needless to say, build to a Knockout Punch whenever you can!

Rating: B+

A little more variety in the fighters would have made this a perfect game. In any case, there are plenty of thrills as you battle for the crown, and the cartridge comes as close to putting you in a boxing match as a Game Boy game can get.

HYPER LODE RUNNER

Type: Maze-style chase

Object: It's the 23rd century, and the evil Red Lord of
Darkness has conquered the world. In order to over-
throw him, you must journey through catacombs to
find hidden Gold that will finance a revolt. While
thus engaged, you must defeat the Cyborg Zombies
commanded by the Red Lord's subordinate, General
Zod—couldn't they have picked a name that *wasn't*
made famous by the Superman saga?

Hero: Your Lode Runner can walk, climb Ladders,
and, most importantly, dig.

Villains: The Zombies can walk, climb Ladders, and
kill you with their touch.

Points: Acquiring Gold gets you points, as does slaying
Zombies.

Strategy: The game is so complex that a review of every level is not possible. However, here are a number of important general tips. For one thing, if you dig a Pit and a Zombie falls in, the dimwit will rise again . . . unless you walk away and suddenly return. He'll descend and be swallowed up. Try it in Level One: when the game starts, dig a Pit to your right—don't move, just dig—walk over the Zombie when it falls in, stand on its head with just your right foot until the creature starts to wriggle, then hurry up the Ladder. Hurry back down again after the Zombie begins to emerge. It'll retreat into the Pit and be swallowed up for good. This tactic works all over the place where there are Ladders; it's great for those areas where you can't afford the luxury of running far ahead of a Zombie and digging the Pit early—so it'll close up as soon as the Zombie falls in, six seconds after being dug. Your timing has to be precise for this to work.

Don't hesitate to use Zombies' heads when you have to. For example, it's the only way to get to the Gold in Level Two.

Another neat trick is to lure a Zombie to a spot where another is standing: it'll be paralyzed. For example, on Level One, in the two-Gold section of Bricks in the upper right, trap a Zombie in the right-side Gold niche, lure another Zombie over and, standing on the right side of the Wall, clear away all the Bricks to the upper left and above the trapped Zombie—three Bricks in all. The Zombie newcomer will walk over . . . and freeze to the upper left of the previously trapped Zombie. When the Bricks rematerialize, it'll die. The danger with this tactic is that, in the heat of combat, you don't always choose your spots with care: Zombies can walk over each others' heads to get across Pits—though they can't stand on them and remain there—so make sure there's nowhere else for the second Zombie to walk when you lure it over.

It will seem, to many, that it's impossible to get in and out of some sections. Not true! Look, for example, at the Level One cache of Gold, bottom right. To get the two piles, stand on top of the Bricks, facing left. Dig up the left Brick first, the right second, drop down, dig the Brick to your lower right, run in and get the Gold, then dig up the Brick to the lower left . . . all of this before the Bricks rematerialize and trap you inside. On that same level get the Gold in the niches on the upper right by standing on the Ladder and shooting the Bricks away one at a time as you move down, ducking in and getting the Gold before you're locked in.

Finally, put the game on pause to study each of the rooms and possible solutions; it's tough to do that while Zombies are chasing you!

By going to the level screen and pushing the A button, you can select any of the 50 levels. However, you can only go to levels one through 16 without a password. If you want to take a look at any of the other levels, use the A button to get to the number, then input this code: QM-0388.

Rating: A

There are people who absolutely *hate* this game. Even if digging out the Gold weren't tough enough, there are those very tenacious Zombies running around. While *Hyper Lode Runner* is definitely not for beginners, it's a corker of a game for experienced players.

MR. CHIN'S GOURMET PARADISE

Type: Level-to-level chase

Object: Mr. Chin loves food, and Peaches are a favorite. The tastiest Peaches in the world are Momos—ambulatory forms that are poisonous in their natural state and must be blasted to be purified and, thus, eaten. Armed with a DEMOE Beam, Mr. Chin sets about doing just that.

Hero: Mr. Chin can run, jump, and fire his Beam. The Beam can only be fired when *two* are placed on the ground; the Momos are turned to Peaches only when they're caught between the two terminals. Mr. Chin can also break Blocks to collect power-ups as described in the instruction booklet. Be careful, though: the power-ups vanish after a few seconds. Power-ups are *usually* but not *always* in the same spot, or thereabouts, from game to game. Therefore, it's a good idea to clear a stage of all but one Peach and go around smashing Blocks to see if you can find a one-up. (Note: stand in the middle of a Beam and you can't be hurt!)

Villains: The walking Momos will destroy Mr. Chin if
they touch him. Momos can't walk over a Beam
once it's placed on the ground. Moments after a
Momo has been transformed, more arrive.

Points: Strictly speaking, they're *calories,* and you collect 'em by eating Peaches and smashing Floor
Blocks. Catch more than one in rapid succession
and the point total doubles—200, 400, 800, and so
on. After you've cleared each stage, you'll have a
few seconds before the next one begins: use that
time to smash Blocks and earn points!

Strategy: The name of the game is *containment:* you
have to herd the Momos together through strategic
placement of the Beam and Walls. Once you've
gathered a group of Momos, use your head (literally) to bash Floors above the "corral" and drop
other Momos into the trap. When you have enough,
get under the Floor beside the Wall—that is, the
side opposite the Beam—knock a hole in it, leap up,
and place a Beam there to fry all the occupants.
Obviously, the more you can trap, the more you can
eat at once, and the more points you will get. Make
a large corral, if possible; you don't want to make
the corral *so* tight that there's no room for the
Momos to roam. Do so and there won't be room for
you to get in on the other side and place a Beam
there! (That's not a problem if you can find a Bomb,
which'll turn all your captives to Peaches.) Don't
overlook the Pipes, which let you move from one
side of the screen to another. Just don't forget that
Momos can do this too, so try to seal it off from
them. Lastly, don't rush ahead to scoop up Peaches
on the top Floor of any level: in the early phases of

each stage, except Stage One, a new Momo will arrive to replace every Peach you eat. It's a good idea to lay down a Beam on one side of a Floor before gathering up metamorphosed Peaches: that way, all you have to do is race around to the other side and put down another Beam to sizzle the new Momos after they've dropped in. Remember, however: if you use a Beam to trap a Momo—say, to the right of it—then put down another Beam to zap Momos to the left of that first Beam, the Beams will disappear and you'll free the Momo that was imprisoned on the right.

Restaurant by restaurant, here's how to start making headway in the game:

Stage One: Put the beam down as soon as the Momos hit the Floor to your left. You'll get most of the Momos.

Stage Two: Drop down to the right, wait until some Momos have fallen, then—facing left—put down a Beam and nail them. If any have escaped, put down another Beam, descend to the Pipe, emerge at the top, head left, and put a Beam across from the other. You'll get the remaining Momos in one blast. You can also go Bomb-hunting in the Floor above the Pipe, just to the right of same. For Gyoza, smash the fat Wall on which the top Floor rests, just left of center.

Bonus Stage: If you want it easy, just stand on the upper left top of the N, facing left, and collect Peaches. Otherwise, make a counterclockwise run to the left across the top of the screen, then concentrate on the Staircase on the far right and the Ledge at the top. Experienced players may wish to start by smashing some strategic Blocks, thus dumping the Momos to the Floor.

Stage Three: Drop at once, so you're beneath the third Floor from the bottom on the far right—in other words, on the tail end of the Z-shaped Wall. Jump up and bash the Blocks for a Bomb, then collect whatever Peaches you can before more Momos descend. Put a Beam on the top Floor, right side, to transform the new arrivals. If you miss any, lure them to the bottom Floor. Look for a Gyoza in the top Floor just right of center!

Stage Four: Go to the Floor directly below you and trap the Momos with a Beam in the center and another on whichever side you can get to. If any escape, drop to the bottom Floor as often as necessary and use the Ledges above to get back up and place your Beams.

Bonus Stage: Just keep diving down the Pipe and coming back to the top. Stay out of the niche in the top left; you'll waste time getting back up the Staircase. (If you're feeling fast and adventurous, go under the niche, smash the Floor, and let the Peaches drop down on you.)

Stage Five: Face left and put a Beam down at once to cream the Momos, then rush off the left side. Come back to the top via the Pipe. More Momos will have appeared: put a Beam in the center, then deal with one side of Momos. The Beams will disappear after they've discharged, so repeat to get the remaining Peach people. More will drop, so you'll have to corral them on top one more time. If all else fails, break the vertical Wall just to the right of center, or the one to the right of that. You'll usually find a Bomb in the fourth Block up.

Stage Six: This level is a mess . . . er, *Mesh*. The Momos will drop through the opening in the Mesh above you, so do the following: run back and forth on the Floor, putting down a Beam, waiting on the other side for a Momo to drop, Peachifying it, putting down a Beam, rushing to the other side, and repeating.

Bonus Stage: This is a rerun of the first Bonus Stage. Again, stand on the upper left point of the N.

Stage Seven: Plant a Beam and then drop all the way to the bottom. Smash the Blocks overhead: they're of no use to you as Ledges, but the power-ups will help. As soon as you get a Gyoza or Bomb, drop down the Pipe and put a Beam on the other side at the top. Repeat, this time getting the power-up you didn't uncover before. You only need to do this twice to clear the stage. If you fail to get the power-ups, you're going to have to travel via Pipe when the coast is clear, and leap the Momos above to plant your Beams.

Stage Eight: Your best bet for this stage is to pick them off on the bottom, occasionally shuttling to the top to set up Beams there—electrifying the Momos that fall through the Pipe. Face the corners, on the bottom, if you need protection, and leap onto the Ledges in both corners to get away.

Bonus Stage: Same as the second Bonus Stage—the one after Stage Four.

Stage Nine: Actually, it's Stage One all over again, with more Momos. And so the game goes.

Rating: B—

Like *Godzilla,* this one's going to surprise adults: you've got to think fast to win. However, there's too little diversity, and once you get the hang of things, you won't find it as much fun. Unlike *Godzilla,* the music is fine . . . though the sound effects are awfully screechy. A continue mode would have been nice: beginners will be frustrated each time they're sent back to the first stage.

MOTOCROSS
MANIACS

Type: Racing game

Object: To drive your motorbike through eight increasingly difficult courses, completing two laps on each.

Hero: Your bike can accelerate, do midair Loops, or race on its back tire—aka popping wheelies, or just plain "popwheelies"—and collect sundry power-ups which are explained in the instructions.

Villains: Just the track, Jack, and its various obstacles. These include other bikers in certain games . . . but in any case, you still have to beat the clock, not the bikers.

Points: None; the race is against time.

Strategy: Each player comes up with his or her own way of working the controls. However, the one that seems most successful is to play with the thumb either pressing down on the center of the pad, shifting up and down or side to side as necessary, or flat on its side, also shifting. This works better, for the most part, than playing with a fingertip. For the A and B buttons the middle and index fingers of the other hand work best there.

Here are general tips:

• Try to come out of Loops on your back tire, then shift quickly to both tires. The back tire acts like a brake; otherwise, the momentum may send you forward too quickly and you'll take a spill.

• Hit Rocks while riding on your back wheel, simultaneously giving your Bike a burst of Nitro: this will carry you over the Rock and onto and over a second Rock, if there's one beyond.

• When power-ups are suspended above you, consider getting them by doing a Loop. That will buy you a little extra time in the air, giving you a chance to nab the power-up then have a look at the terrain on which you'll be landing. Doing Loops will also allow you to grab invisible power-ups—which appear more or less regularly.

• Invisible power-ups are generated at random by the game chip. However, when they appear, they can always be found by doing a Loop in the following places, among others:

One: over the first Hop-A-Longs, between the two Signs after the Ramp, and above the Hop-A-Longs right after that.

Two: above the first Hop-A-Longs and after the Sign on the upper roadway beyond.

Three: on the first upper roadway and after the first Sign on the higher roadway—the one after the Loop.

Four: above the first set of Hop-A-Longs and on the second high road after that, just beyond the Sign.

Five: over the second set of Hop-A-Longs, just before the Sign.

Six: between the high Ramps with the sign between them—you reach them using the Takeoff Ramp on the ground, located just after the N—and on the first elevated roadway that has a Rock and both the Go Sign and a Loop Sign on it (do a Loop off the Rock to get it).

Seven: between the two upraised Hop-A-Longs—following the first bunch of Rocks. (Note: on this level, when you reach the Loop with the T and N to the left, use two Nitro boosters to get to the N. After that, hit the Rock on your back wheel, punch in a Nitro, and use the Rock to launch you at the roadway above.)

Eight: there are none on this level.

• Don't forget that you can do forward Loops, driving *into* the direction you're going, as though you were doing a forward somersault. These will get you to the ground faster than backward Loops.

• When doing "island hopping"—landing on clear stretches between Macho Dirt—either do forward Loops to get over them, and/or touch down on your back tire so you can take right off again.

• One of the neatest tricks you can perform in *Motocross Maniacs* is to take the rather unorthodox "subterranean route." Starting with the Loop that's nearly halfway into the first lap of 2A—the one with the Macho Dirt on the left and a ramp near the right—lay into the B button three or four times over as you circle the Loop. When you come down, you'll literally be driven into the Dirt: you'll hit so hard you'll be half buried, which will allow you to continue unobstructed to the end! You won't be able to collect any of the power-ups . . . but then, you won't need to!

Rating: B+

The race theme isn't for everyone; you really don't need to use your brain at all. But the game is fast, there's no room at all for sloppy playing—no second chance at missed power-ups or sections of roadway —and there are a lot of tricky maneuvers to master. Once you do that, you face the task of beating your previous time, giving you a reason to go back to the cartridge again and again.

PIPE DREAM

Type: Maze-type puzzle game

Object: You've got a supply of Pipes, and a flood about to happen! Your mission: to place as many Pipes down as you can, staying ahead of the so-called flooz flood for as long as possible.

Hero: Your Pipes come in these basic shapes: four kinds of right angle or corner pieces—with one of each, you could form a square—horizontal and vertical straight lengths, and crossbar Pipes. Pipes can be placed anywhere on the grid and can be "blasted" by superimposing another one. You can lay Pipe on the grid expecting to link up with it later. There are also Blocks that must be worked around: if the flooz hits them, the game ends.

Villains: The flooz begins flowing after a set period; after that, it can't be stopped and it just gets faster.

Points: For each section of Pipe you put down to control the flow, you're rewarded; your score is diminished for each section of Pipe you put down that you don't use. The only exception to this is any section of Pipe that intersects a flooz-filled Pipe.

Strategy: Every screen is different, and your placement of each Pipe makes every game unique. Here, then, are general tactics:

• Since the name of the game is to stay ahead of the flooz, that's your top priority. If you can't use a piece, put it *near* the end of your Pipe system: if you can get to it soon, it'll buy you time. If not, you can always blast it when you get there.

• Look at the way the Pipes are laid out on the left. If there are any patterns you can use, put them down as is to save time.

• Stay away from the sides as much as possible: you'll only box yourself in. Not necessarily immediately—but later, when you may have to move around the initial structure you built. Leave at least enough room to snake straight sections of Pipe along the sides.

• If things are getting crowded and you keep getting Pipe pieces you don't want—especially in the later stages—start blasting them. Why have extra Pipe deducted from your score? Wherever possible in these instances, place matching sections over existing sections near your position—or simply over the last segment of Pipe you don't need: you'll want to stay there in case a piece you need arrives rather than rush all over.

• At the beginning of a stage plan your approach to the Reservoir or Bonus Pipe after taking a quick look at the pieces coming up.

• If you don't know what to do with a right angle Pipe, put it around a Block. You'll probably need it there eventually!

• Lay down Pipe to *get you away from the starting point!* If you can't use any of the first few pieces, scatter them nearby where they *might* be useful. Better to leave a few unconnected Pipes than to be floozed out early on.

• Where the game has an End Piece, keep an eye on that and, indeed, place Pipe there when you can to build toward where you are.

• Try to get yourself beside a Tunnel: there, you usually have the option to use more pieces, since you can build the Pipe system in the section where you are, or cut through the Tunnel and continue elsewhere.

• If you're waiting for a piece, just stay in the spot where it's needed and keep blasting Pipes over and over until—hopefully!—you get it.

• When you get the One Way Pipes, place them on the side of a Reservoir on a side opposite the direction from which you're coming. You'll certainly want to make for the Reservoir and, so doing, you'll have to leave it; the One Way Pipe is a step in that direction.

• Leave the grids at the ends of the Reservoirs clear, for obvious reasons.

• You have *two* straight pieces you can use—the straight one and the Loop Pipe—so consider the odds of getting those when you plan your run toward an End Piece. For instance, it's a good idea to leave yourself a place to make a straight run near the end, since you'll be racing to put down pieces fast—not just to control the flooz, but to meet your quota of Pipe!

• Passwords bring you to the levels after every fourth level. Here are those codes:

HAHA (5)
GRIN (9)
REAP (13)
SEED (17)
GROW (21)
TALL (25)
YALI (29)

After winning 32, you'll get the following prompt: TRY LAST 4STAGE. This time, at least, you get to *see* the darn screen when you put it on pause! (There is, alas, no code to bring you here.)

Rating: A
This is one of those "you'll never get bored of them" cartridges, which is also good for players of all ages and experience levels. Innovative and—you'll pardon the expression—a *blast!*

QUARTH

Type: *Tetris*-type game

Object: At the controls of your ship Blockbuster in the Quarthdome, you are besieged by blocklike Shapes falling from the sky. Armed with square blocks (Quarths) of your own, you must fill the descending Shapes before they touch you. If you make them completely square or rectangular before they touch you, they vanish. If not, your Blockbuster will be crushed.

Hero: Landlocked in the Quarthdome, you can slide from side to side and fire blocks. You have the ability to change the blocklike Shape by adding to the existing structure any way you wish as it falls. However, before it reaches you, that new Shape you've created must still be rendered fully square or rectangular. You win various power-ups by blasting exceedingly large Shapes: these are described in the instruction booklet. If you want, you can speed up the descent of the Shapes (push up on the pad) . . . and then go have your head examined!

Villains: The blocklike Shapes come down in the same
pattern from game to game—though each level is
different from every other level—and are the only
foe.

Points: Each Quarth you place in a completed square
or rectangle earns points. Bonus points are awarded
at the end of each round, determined by the number
of Quarths that hit their targets.

Strategy: Since the game changes entirely depending
upon how you confront each Shape, here are general tactics:

• Play the game with your middle finger on the A
button and your index finger on the B button—reverse if you're a lefty. In the later stages you'll want
to be ready to hit the panic button and call for a
power-up at a moment's notice!

• Keep this in mind if you're hesitant to use power-ups: you can use a power-up to help you tackle a
difficult Shape and, by beating it, win back a power-up—possibly a more powerful one than you sacrificed.

• Not only must you finish the Shapes off, but quite
often you have to do so in a certain order. Some are
taller than others and will reach you faster; other
Shapes are between you and Shapes behind them,
meaning they must be removed before you can get
to the others.

• This rule applies to whatever round you're on: if
there's nothing else right behind a falling Shape,

load it up with as many Quarths as possible. Migh·
as well earn those power-ups when you can!

• If you're working on filling up the last column o·
a Shape, and it's frightfully close, simply pour or
the Quarths! In other columns you have to be careful not to overload a column . . . or that becomes
the new configuration of the Shape. When the last
column is filled, though, the Shape disintegrates.

• Leave the pad set on whatever power-up you
might need next. All you have to do, then, is engage
the B button, rather than go searching for the
power and *then* hit the button.

• While Shapes are disintegrating, you can't fire
through them. Even if the next Shape you want to
attack is behind it, don't sit there waiting: go somewhere else and get a few Quarths placed until the
crumbling Shape is gone.

• On any of the wide Shapes, work from side to side,
leaving no gaps in the middle. The less shifting
around you have to do, the more time you can spend
firing! This is especially important in later rounds,
when the Shapes come at you more quickly and
thickly!

• When you get flat Shapes—that is, the ones that
look like flat lines—build them up to a relatively
high height. Then, if you think you can handle it,
throw on an extra layer or two of Quarths. Putting
the extra few on at the end makes more sense than
loading them on in the beginning: the pressure isn't
as great!

• Also regarding those flat Shapes: the tendency is to drop across them, laying on the same number of Quarths as you sweep from one side to the other. Don't . . . unless they're really close. You can load four different vertical rows on each—for example, really pile them on one of the flat Shapes to get a power-up, then blow away the others with a row just one Quarth deep.

• Sound is a great asset in the game. When filling up a Shape with several columns, *listen* to the number of Quarths you have fired. If you know, for instance, that you put seven Quarths in one column, count out seven for the next—or six if there was already one there; you get the point. You don't actually have to *see* the column filled up to know that you've done so. This allows you to move on to another Shape sooner.

• Load a few Quarths onto emerging L Shapes— they're L's with *very* long stems, which are all you see for a while—but don't load on *too* many: you don't know how long the thing is to begin with and, again, it's easier to add a couple of Quarths onto a nearly finished Shape than to have to pile 'em on in a frantic fight for survival—though those can be pretty darn exciting, *n'est ce pas?*

• Don't think about adding onto *anything* on 3–9: just shoot those suckers as they descend, or your stay in the arena will be brief. (On this level, don't wait until the bases of the first of the L Shapes becomes visible. Even though they're the tallest Shapes, and will reach you first, you're wasting time by waiting! Go to the sides and take out what's visible there! Besides, those L Shapes need just one column to complete them, meaning that you can fire fast without counting.)

• On 3–9, when the "Pipe Organ" arrangement of L Shapes appears, you have no choice but to take them out by shifting all the way from the outer left (or right) to the outer right (or left). It's a lot of running . . . but it *can* be done.

• In the later levels especially, when the air is full of Shapes, try to position yourself strategically so that you can fire at the next Shape without moving. For example, destroy Shapes that are between you and L Shapes so that when you've fired your last shot and the Shape vanishes, all you need to do is keep firing to hit the L Shape's empty side.

Rating: B+

What a super, underrated game! Okay, there are no monsters with gruesome kissers, or spaceships blasting away. *Quarth* lacks personality, and that makes the slower sections a tad dull. But the game can get really exciting, and the music and sound effects are first-rate.

SERPENT

Type: *Qix*-style competition

Object: In the far future, contestants slip into Vehicles and race around a track, trying to cut off or box in an adversary. You are one such actioneer, ready to battle the computer Vehicle or another player.

Hero: Your Vehicle can move in any direction and, by leaving a Trail that traces a Box in the arena, may cause various power-ups to appear. To claim them, you must run over them. You can also run over power-ups your adversary has generated—and vice versa!

Villains: In addition to another Vehicle, your enemy is the same process that causes power-ups to appear: by creating a Box, you might also generate power-downs. Obviously, if you don't want one, don't run over it!

Points: Each victory is worth a point; seven points wins the level.

Strategy: Every move you make changes the game, so only general tactics apply:

• Even though you've already got a particular weapon, grab another one if it appears: you don't want your enemy getting it!

• If you accidentally box yourself in, move as little as you can, stop until you've blinked a bit, move slightly, etc. In short, stay alive: you never know when your opponent is going to make a fatal turn!

• When you see a Clear Missile, drop everything and get it. That's the most effective weapon you can acquire.

• If you get *hit* with a Clear Missile, head for open territory and turn away from your enemy wherever she or he moves. Otherwise, you're finished.

• A tack that usually manages to get things going against the computer Vehicle: if it comes down and cuts to the left right away, drive up and, just past the midway point, swing to the right, cut up almost at once, then drive left at the top. You'll almost always be able to catch the computer Vehicle in a Box on top.

• If your enemy is trapped in a Box of her or his own making, hurry over and reinforce it with your own Trail.

• In your haste to trap your enemy, don't make a Box that leaves your foe with room to move inside the Box, while you're pinned with a Trail overhead and a Trail in front! Your time may run out before his or hers does.

• If your opponent creates two sides of a Box using his or her own Trail—especially a small Box—rush over and try to form the other two sides, then quickly reinforce the ones he or she made. The other Vehicle usually won't be able to get out in time.

• Don't inadvertently free your foe from a trap by moving ahead: the section of your Trail that is holding him or her in may be removed when you continue. If you must move, drive up against a section of wall or Trail, stand still for a few moments, move again just a bit, stand still, and so on.

• By the same token, if you've been cornered by your opponent's tail, don't panic and start roaming around in the Box, surrounding yourself with your own Trail! The other Vehicle may move ahead and free you!

• If you've accidentally Boxed yourself in with just your tail section—that is, if there's only one layer to the surrounding Box—you can still get out. Simply trace a Trail back and forth along the section of the Box opposite the side from the first outer section you created. With luck, that outside wall will vanish before you do.

Rating: D+

Serpent is like nothing else on the market for Game Boy. Unfortunately, that's a crummo reason to buy it. There are moments when you'll have to do some quick thinking and fast maneuvering. But the graphics are unappealing, the music grating, and overall, the cartridge won't "call" to you to play again and again the way so many others do.

SNOOPY'S MAGIC SHOW

Type: Blockout maze-type game

Object: Woodstock and his little bird friends have been captured, and it's up to Snoopy to rescue them! Snoopy's brother Spike and some Bouncing Balls are on hand just to make things difficult.

Hero: Snoopy, the venerable *Peanuts* dog, can run, move certain Blocks, bust others, and uncover various power-ups described in the instruction booklet. His one weakness: Balls. Touch one and he's a dead dog.

Villains: Balls ricochet around the mazes; Snoopy dies when hit. However, a Ball can be destroyed if Snoopy gets a P and hits it within five seconds.

Points: Score 'em for saving Woodstocks. You're awarded a time bonus, so the faster you finish, the more points you receive!

Strategy: There are over 100 levels; here's the level-by-level lowdown for the first 20 screens of the game, with the passwords and tips, where appropriate.

1NWQ (2) ("one")
70BT (3) ("zero")
104A (4) ("zero")
4N44 (5)
1NX2 (6) ("one"): When you do this level, go for the upper right then upper left Woodstocks, since the Balls tend to bounce in other directions. Get the lower left one next; you can usually do this all in one swift run.

105H (7) ("one" and "zero"): Head bottom left then top left to start; the Ball almost always goes to the right. Scurry to the right wherever the Ball isn't (duh!), then grab the last Woodstock when the coast is clear.

10XD (8) ("one" and "zero"): Do the sections in logical progression—lower right, top right, top left, lower left—but don't hit the One Way Squares until the Ball is bouncing away from wherever you'll end up!

1N1C (9) ("ones"): Since the Balls converge on the lower right, go to the upper left, then upper right—ducking into the doorway in the top corridor if a Ball is bouncing your way. Get the other two by following the One Way Squares when the coast is clear.

1N10 (10) ("ones" and "oh"): Get the bird in the upper left, then the lower left. By this time, the Ball on your side will almost always have Teleported over. Teleport yourself—after first making sure there isn't a Ball about to hit the Teleporter on the other side—and nab the Woodstock on the top right. (If the Ball *is* near the Teleporter, it may bounce in and come to your side. Use the Blocks on the left for protection if it does, and slip into the Teleporter when you can.) Head to the Woodstock on the bottom when you can make a dash to the Blocks down there. Use them as protection from the Ball while you grab the bird.

HOO7 (11) ("zero" "oh"): Go at once to the upper right—if you stand still, the Ball will hit you—come down in the top/middle, cut to the far left, and get the Woodstock in the upper left. Do the lower right and lower left in that order, with stop-and-go movements to avoid the Ball.

10EI (12) ("one" "zero" "capital I"): Rush into the center section, then out the upper right to get the Woodstock. Push down the rightmost Block on top for a Teleporter. It'll heave you back to the upper left: rush in and down to the Woodstock on the lower left, come up and get the one in the center, then claim the one in the lower right.

ONBV (13) ("oh"): The easiest way to win this section is to trap the Ball. Just make sure you don't trap it with a Woodstock: once you close off a corridor, you may not be able to get back in! There's a Clock in the second Block from the top of the horizontal column on the right, and a Teleporter above the *e* in "pause" —pause the game to see where. Another way to get at the birds is to push a Block above them and to the side of that one, creating a little pocket you can walk into.

1N1B (14) ("ones"): There's a Clock in the Block above you. This one seems tough, but it's simple, really. Just wait until the Disappearing Blocks appear. When they're in front of the One Way Squares, you can cross *against* the direction indicated by the arrow!

C01X (15) ("zero" "one"): Stopping to let the Ball bounce by, here are the One Way Squares to follow: go left, up, and get the two birds; go down to the right-pointing arrow on the right, then up the one on the far right. Get the bird in the top right, then head left, down at the arrow to the left of center, left at the next One Way Square below you pointing in that direction, and then up.

10I1 (16) ("one" "zero" "capital I" "one"): Ride the One Way Squares on the left side and, while the Disappearing Square is next to the Woodstock in the upper left, get 'im. While they're still there, you should be able to ride the right side arrows down to the bird there. If not, do so anyway and wait for the Disappearing Blocks to return. Get the Woodstock in the lower right. Go to the lower left and wait there, then ride the arrows to the upper right.

CZ10 (17) ("one" "zero"): Ride the One Way Square down, then move in a counterclockwise direction. You should be able to get around the screen almost without stopping for a Ball!

XZ2Q (18): Head left, blast the Fragile Block to get the bird, go up to the right, blast the Block there for that bird, come down, and go right to get the Woodstock in the lower right corner. Head left, riding the One Way Squares up and then right, walk left at the top of the screen, and get the bird in the upper left.

1QET (19) ("one"): First of all, there's a Clock in the Fragile Block, upper right—just in case you want it. To get the birds: go right and down the center, blast the Fragile Block and get the Woodstock on the bottom. Destroy the Fragile Block below to get the Woodstock on the left, then grab the two birds on the right. All you have to do is evade the Balls . . . an easy task!

XQ1A (20) ("one"): Wend your way through the Blocks to get the birds on the lower right and upper left, in that order. Then, using the Blocks for protection, make your way to either corner in turn and wait: when the Balls bounce away, move in for the last two Woodstocks.

Some additional passwords: VZY4, XZ12 ("one"), 1QEH ("one"), XQ1D ("one"), 2ZVC, XZ1O ("one" "oh"), ZQJ7, XQSI ("capital I"), XZ1V ("one"), XZUB, 2QOX ("oh"), XQ11 ("ones"), ZYU0 ("zero"), BYBQ, TTOT ("oh"), BTBA, BY14 ("one"), BY12 ("one"), VTNH, BTND, HYOC ("oh"), BYYO ("oh"), and OT17 ("oh" "one").

Rating: A

Everyone's going to have a ball with this one! Fun for youngsters and an intelligent puzzler for veteran videogamers, with a quick pace and surprisingly different screens. And, for once, a licensed character actually looks like it's supposed to. Note: the title screen refers to the game as *Snoopy Magic Show*. We've gone with the name on the box and instructions for our heading because the other one makes no sense! Pity Kemco can make such a terrific game but can't get the name straight . . .

SOLARSTRIKER

Type: Space shoot-'em-up

Object: It's those old rats from Reticulon, come to earth in the year 2159 intent on conquest. From earth's "megabase" on the moon, you must fly out and meet the enemy fleet.

Hero: Your ship, *SolarStriker,* can fly anywhere on the screen while firing toward the top at the oncoming enemy. You'll encounter power-ups (P) along the way; collecting them boosts your ship's Missile levels. If you perish having collected a number of P's, you'll return with half of them.

Villains: The enemy ships move in different ways and fire various projectiles. These vessels are pictured in the instruction booklet.

Points: The points awarded for destroying each ship are described in the instructions.

Strategy: There are a few tactics to use in this game. In the end, though, everything's going to depend upon the player's speed and reflexes.

Strategically, the bottom line with this game is simple, and it's just that: stay on the very bottom. Fire away as ships emerge: your projectiles will hit most of them before they can disgorge bombs at you, and you can easily evade those few explosives. Moreover, if you're low on the screen, you can get off another shot should the first one miss. If a ship *does* get by you, rise up slightly from the bottom to let it pass under you, then settle back down and continue firing. Whatever you do, if a single ship gets away, *don't* chase it: you'll only end up into a corner, a sitting duck for the ships you ignored while pursuing just one!

Stage One: This is typical of what you'll have to face—and it's the only one that goes *slowly* enough for us to point out valuable maneuvers. You'll use variations of these throughout the game . . . only faster! To begin with, just shift from side to side, covering the center third of the screen, to deal with the Rotomechs. When the Protodroids arrive, go to the left side to destroy the wave there, then to the right side. Shortly after the first P, the Harriers arrive from alternate sides: sweep from left to right to get them. Cruisers join the fray shortly after the second P, descending in columns from the right and then the left, after which the others make return appearances. The Stage Boss, Epikhan, descends straight down the center: still on the very bottom, keep shooting up at it while dodging its waves of projectiles. The way to beat it is to watch the bombs, not the ship: move to one side in several jerking steps to avoid the wave moving that way, then to the other side to miss that wave. Even without looking at the Boss, a steady fire will destroy it.

Stage Two: The fun starts with a few Rotomechs to lull you into a state of complacent familiarity, after which Pinchers charge with their halting attacks. But the Rotomechs return—did they have a sale on these things at the intergalactic munitions plant?—along with Arrowheads. The boss here, Destructor, moves in a figure eight while launching Bubble Bombs, which can be destroyed for points . . . and survival! Shoot when the boss is at the top of the screen, then get above it so you'll have room to maneuver.

Stage Three: It's a Skimbot attack to start things rolling; knit between the rows, blasting the vessels as they appear. Zigzags follow, weaving in and out; slide left and right under their ranks. When the Macks show up, they won't fire at once: that'll give you time to get over and pick off these powerful adversaries. Terra Cannons are plentiful and up next: you *can* rush from side to side and try to get them all, but it's suggested that you stick to one side, blasting ahead while noting the patterns of fire from the other and avoiding it. Ultra Crusher is the boss and will start firing at once as it moves in to—well, crush you. Get up close, fast, and get in your shots while dodging its fire. Get behind it when it descends and under it again when it rises.

Stage Four: Vexors welcome you by approaching, retreating, and zipping over again. You'll have to go from side to side to get them, avoiding their fire as you do. Ditto Batwings. Shoot ahead of the next ships, Warhawks, and let them fly into your fire. The sub-boss is Omniquad, a tough cookie: you'll have to get to the central computer by shooting away the surrounding Pods and avoiding its fire. Circle it, concentrating on one Pod at a time until it's destroyed. This not only allows you to fight with economy, it lets you create a "safe zone" on that side of the Omniquad.

Specific advice won't help you hereafter: the game is so fast you'll just be shooting and ducking wildly —sometimes blindly, just *hoping* you don't get hit— especially on the boss levels. You'll have to keep up a constant stream of fire while executing lightning-fast dodges to get around them and/or duck their projectiles.

Rating: C

This is one of the oldest kinds of Nintendo games, harking back to *Alpha Mission* for the NES. There have been virtually no creative embellishments: the enemies are pretty faceless and, except for their moves, there are too few variations or surprises. Also, the power-ups are pretty unsatisfying, and there are *no* warps or continues—which can get frustrating. Good for fans who thrive on fast play of this sort.

SPIDER-MAN

Type: Web-'em-up and wall-crawling

Object: Spider-Man's wife, Mary-Jane, has been kid-
napped, and the hero must battle ordinary criminals and master criminals as he roams the streets,
walls, and rooftops of New York in search of her.

Hero: Spider-Man can walk, jump, crouch, kick,
punch, shoot debilitating Webs, climb walls, and
swing from strands of Web. Spider-Man gets three
lives in each game, the game continuing exactly
where the last Spider-Man died. You can lose all
three Spideys and continue—but only three times.

Villains: Some just walk along unarmed, others fire at
Spider-Man, a few slink up from under manholes
and grab him, a few Clubbers poke from windows
and swing clubs at the hero, and so forth. The master criminals—Mysterio, Hobgoblin, the Scorpion,
the Rhino, Dr. Octopus, and Venom—are not only

extremely tough to kill, they come armed with special powers.

Points: The player earns points by slaying foes, starting at 80 for killing an ordinary criminal or Gunman, to 100 for stomping a manhole down on a foe or punching out someone's lights in a window, to 200 for catching whatever a foe drops, to tens of thousands of points for destroying a master criminal. A more important goal than all of these, however, is Hamburgers, which pop up now and then. Each time Spidey eats one, he can restore a portion of whatever energy he lost while fighting enemies. Note: you can still grab a Hamburger even if most of it has scrolled off the screen.

Strategies: In general, use your Webbing as *infrequently* as possible: you'll need it for the confrontations with the master criminals. Use it to cross otherwise impassable areas . . . but then drop down and duke it out with your ordinary foes. Also, try and use the kick rather than the punch as much as possible. To kick you have to crouch, and that's a safer position than standing!

Mysterio: Walk along, but when you see the first group of ruffians—before you reach the first Manhole—let them come to you. Crouch, kick, and then continue along. After the second Manhole, you'll come to a Window with a bully inside. Web him, drop down, and rush onto the Crate with the Gunman behind it. Hop the bullets, grab the Hamburger from the Window, then hop behind the felon and punch him. (You can get the Gunman first, but you run the risk of scrolling the Hamburger off the left side.) At the following Window with Clubbers, wait until they've swung—you can't be hurt when the Club is down—then jump up and kick them. Deal with the next Gunman as you did the first. At the next Hamburger Window, go past it, then turn and get it by leaping to the left with a long jump. (If you long-jump to the *right,* you may land within the deadly perimeter of the Manhole.) Watch out for the thug that'll attack between this Manhole and the one right after it. There's a Hamburger in the second Window of the next building: long-jump onto the Crates, then leap to the left to get it. Just make sure you leap off *quickly,* since a Clubber is in the Window above. There's another Hamburger in the next Window; the Gunman shooting to the right makes it tough to get. Hop to the top of the Crates between bullets, leap the next one that comes your way, jump for the Hamburger, get back on the Crates between bullets, then attack. No new challenges until you meet Mysterio. Don't bother Webbing him: get in close and kick him. Just stay out of the way of the "Clouds" that precede his materialization. They'll rob of you of your strength faster'n you can say "Stan Lee!"

Hobgoblin: The first stage is climbing the Wall, and it's pretty simple. As far as falling debris goes, the safest place is just to the left of the center row of Windows. You'll have to watch out for a few Clubbers, but you'll want them for points, and besides, you can kill them: you can't kill the stuff falling from the Rooftop! Taking this route—with your right hand and foot actually touching the left side of the center Windows—you'll only have to make a few shifts to the left to avoid debris on your way up. Once you get to the Roof, you should have to do very little Webbing—rely mostly on long-jumps to cross from Rooftop to Rooftop, and kicks or punches to beat foes—which is good: you'll need the strands to fight the Hobgoblin. There are a lot of Gunmen on the Rooftops, so be prepared to duck, and make sure you kill everyone in sight: if you leave any Gunmen behind you, they'll fire at you after you've passed! If you happen to miss one or two, crouch, deal with the guy in front using kicks—thus ducking bullets from behind—then scroll the Gunman to the left off the screen. When Hobgoblin arrives, get rid of his henchman—or else he'll be firing at you while you battle the master criminal—hop to the left Rooftop, face right, and spin Webs at Hobgoblin, knocking him off the screen to the right. He'll return to the left each time; kick him each time he rises up along the right side of the left building—which he does every time—sidestep the Bombs he drops, wait until he shifts to the right, then Web him again. If you're out of Web fluid, you're going to have a tough time beating this fiend with just kicks!

Scorpion: You're atop a moving Train, with Gunmen shooting at you and Bats flying at you. Kick the former—hopping their bullets, as necessary—and leap or punch the latter as you go. Just make sure the Bats don't crowd you to the left and scroll you off the screen! Note the Ledges above you: use them as a sanctuary whenever you can. At the end of the ride, Scorpion will descend on you: he's actually simple to defeat. His tail is deadly, but it is only on one side. The master criminal's other side is completely open. Punch or kick him there and he's doomed.

Rhino: You're in Central Park—though it's anything but relaxing. Deadly Pine Cones fall from trees, Pigeons fly over and drop Eggs . . . and there are more Manholes, Gunmen, and ordinary hoodlums. There is no strategy from this point forward, other than to rely more on Webbing than before to clear a path through the *very* thick crowd of enemies. When you battle Rhino, the key to victory is getting behind him. Leap him when he charges, punch him in the back, leap when he turns, and so on.

Dr. Octopus: The climb up the wall is more or less the same as last time. Take the same tack, though you'll have to rely on your Spidey Sense a *bit* more than before. The Roof is different geographically than the last one, since you'll be doing a lot of your moving and fighting on various Window Ledges. There are also Pigeons here, and you'll have to bop them while you're busy swinging from Webs. There are also collapsible sections of Roof, which you'll recognize by their slightly darker tone. Upon the arrival of Dr. Octopus, get in close and kick or Web him—then jump back. His retractible arms will stretch out and try to grab you. If he succeeds, it's time to hang up those red and blue tights.

Venom: Only quick reflexes and plenty of Web fluid will save you as you walk through the Sewers in search of the head boss. Stay out of the Sewage: not only does it slow you down, but there are Crocodiles hiding in the muck. Watch out for men on the Pipes overhead: go up and kill them rather than wait till they come down. Waiting only gives them more time to fire. Also leap the Drains set in the Wall: the sewage is deadly. Venom is more or less a clone of Spidey: he dangles from his own Web on the left and right side of the screen and shoots the stuff at you. Stay on the high ground (the Platform) on the right when you fight him. Leap or duck his Webs, and

Web him right back the instant he stops firing: not
only will that weaken him, it'll prevent him from
Webbing you! When he comes down on the right
side of the screen, stay as far left on the Platform as
you can, but stick to this tactic.

Rating: B

If you like games of this type, where you march
along shooting and fighting, *Spider-Man* is as chal-
lenging as any Nintendo eight-bit game. Frankly, it
isn't as much fun as *Batman* . . . but then, Spidey
uses more of his powers than Batman does, making
for play-value the other superhero game lacks.

SUPER MARIO LAND

Type: Fantasy quest

Objective: One day a black cloud appeared over Sarasaland and out came the evil Tatanga, conquering the realm and announcing that he would wed its Princess Daisy. But heroic Mario vows to cross the four kingdoms of Sarasaland—Birabuto (World 1), Muda (2), Easton (3), and Chai (World 4), each of which consists of three lesser realms—to rescue Daisy and defeat Tatanga.

Hero: Mario defeats enemies by leaping on top of them or butting them off Blocks. Along the way he can obtain various power-up items. Each Heart gives you an additional Mario; 100 Coins also provides an extra Mario. (Note: most Blocks give one Coin. Some, noted below, give more: how many depends entirely on how fast you repeatedly strike the Block). You can also get Stars, Flowers, and Super Mushrooms. Super Mushrooms increase Mario's size—cause him to become "powered-up" as Super Mario—Flowers enable him to throw Super Balls at foes (only one Super Ball can be on the screen at a time; one Ball kills *both* parts of two-section creatures like Nokobons and Mekabons, while some creatures, like Honen, are impervious to them), and Stars make him invincible for short periods. (You'll know when your invincibility is about to expire: a theme from *Orpheus in the Underworld* plays through twice. When it ends, so does Mario's imperviousness.) Be advised, however, that he's invincible *only* when it comes to enemies: if Mario falls off a Ledge, he'll die. These items are all located inside ? Blocks. Blocks from which Super Mushrooms emerge when Mario is not Super Mario will give forth Flowers when he is. These items remain on-screen for as long as Mario is on that screen. Mario also has a submarine, Marine Pop, and an airplane, Sky Pop. These are used only in Worlds 2/3 and 4/3, respectively. When you fire their guns, no more than three unexploded projectiles can appear on the screen at once.

In some areas, Mario will be breaking walkways for points and power-ups. This will leave holes in the floor. To cross, simply keep the B button pressed down. Mario will walk on air!

If Mario dies at any point in the game, he doesn't lose any of the Coins or points he's amassed, though the next Mario starts back a short distance in *most* cases. (Having said that, in a few sections of the game he actually starts *ahead* of where he died! The Nokobon platform at the end of 2/2 is a rare example.) And while any foes he's killed usually remain dead—the Honen at the start of 2/1 are an exception—the new Mario can get all the ?'s again. Likewise, before Mario enters a Pipe, be certain to collect any Coins or power-ups from ? Blocks to the immediate right of the Pipe. The ? will be replenished when he gets out, allowing him to "double-dip."

Villains: It would be redundant to cite them here. Read all about them as you meet each one in the *Strategy* section below. Keep in mind, however, that any foe that may have been about to attack when Mario entered a Pipe, will be gone when he emerges.

Points: These range from 100 for each little squirt that attacks, to 5000 for the bosses of each level . . . and Tatanga. A Super (powered-up) Mario also earns 50 points for shattering Blocks—normal Mario can't shatter them. Creatures that can detach bodily parts grant more points when killed in one piece than if each section is slain separately—just make sure you *do* kill both parts, however, as the remaining part may regenerate what you destroyed. Points are also awarded for each Coin collected. In every level, you're playing against time, so don't dawdle! However, if you lose track of the time, the music will speed up when you have just 100 seconds left.

Strategy: Each of Sarasaland's worlds is divided into three sections. Here's how to get through them all:

1/1: There's a Coin in the first Block, a power-up in the second, and a Coin in the third. Get on the third Pipe and press down: there's a Coin room inside. Upon emerging, collect a Coin from the Block above. (As noted above, in situations like this, if you get the Coin *before* going into the Pipe, you can hit the Block and collect again when you emerge!) Stop at the foot of the plateau ahead. There's a Chibibo on it, so stand there until the little fellow comes down, then jump on it. When you reach the first row of Blocks, either hurry to the right before the two Chibibos drop from the Ledge, or stay to the left until they emerge from under the row. If *you're* underneath, the Blocks will prevent you from jumping and stomping the creatures, and you'll perish. (Unless, of course, you've shattered the Blocks and can jump up in that narrow channel. However, it's a tricky move and not worth the risk.)

After dispensing with the twerps, get the Coin in the ? above. Beyond the next Pipe is a row of six Blocks. Hop on them, go to the right, then jump down and get the Coins as you fall. If you miss them, get on the ?, smash all the Blocks on the upper left, leap back onto the Pipe—assuming you haven't scrolled it too far left—and try again. (If you fail at this, wait till you get Super Ball power across the Pit, and shoot left to nail the Coins.) When you're underneath the row, collect the Coin from the lonely ?, then jump onto that Block and hit the row above: the second Block from right contains a one-up. Jump onto the row of three Blocks to the right, hop up and hit the ? on top, then leap onto it and get the power-up. (If you're Super Mario, make sure that you don't inadvertently smash the Blocks below the ? before you use them as stepping-stones! Otherwise, you won't be able to get the power-up.)

A Nokobon comes next: jump on it then get away *fast*, or its Bomb will explode. Obtain a Coin from the ? after the Pipe, at which point you'll arrive at three rows of Blocks. None on bottom can be broken, so don't bother trying. Just hop onto the second row, collect Coins from all the top Blocks, drop back down to the bottom row, then butt all the Blocks in the second row for Coins. Leap the Pit: the Pipe there takes you to a Coin room. (Remember: first get the Coin in the ? to the right.) If you're a non–Super Mario, bounce off the ceiling as you go along the bottom tier—that is, press the controller right and keep jabbing the A button repeatedly—this will save a lot of time. When you leave the room, there are Coins in the next two ? Blocks. As soon as the second ? appears, a Fly will come after you. Flies hop, then rest for several seconds: jump on top of them immediately after they hop. Next up is a Pipe to the left of a stack of Blocks. Jump onto the Pipe, use a Super Ball on the Chibibo down there—or jump down on it if you don't have Super Ball power —then hop onto the stack. Wait there, and shoot the Chibibo when it approaches. Now jump and hit the ?, and grab the Star when it floats down. (If you'd hit the ? *before* blasting the second Chibibo, the Star would have drifted down right on top of it. Where would you be then?) Invincible, you can race ahead.

The next row of Blocks is all Coins. If you missed catching the Star, watch out, again, that you don't get trapped underneath as a Chibibo enters from the right. The next two ?'s have Coins. Your Invincibility should carry you through the first Fly that attacks . . . and, if you hurry, the second as well. If not, kill them as before. (Regarding the first Fly: if you've run out of invincibility, you can stand atop the Pipe. When the Fly jumps up at you, it will *usually* self-destruct.) Get the ?, a Coin.

The Sphinx on the other side of the Pit can't hurt you, so just hop over. Above it you'll find a row in which the last (unmarked) Block contains many Coins: again, you can get up to 15 if you strike *fast*. Just keep butting the Block until it's empty. At the pyramidlike structure made of Blocks, get the lower row of Coins first. (If you get the upper row first, the screen will scroll to the left so far that you may not be able to get back down to them.) If you're Super Mario and, thus, oversized, simply stand on the first Block on the left of the lowest Coin row—*not* the Block jutting to the left, below it—squat, and fire a Super Ball at the Coins. The Ball will collect them for you! Go up to the second row and squat *squarely* on the Block at the beginning of the second tier of Coins. Fire a Super Ball to collect the Coins. If you have trouble with that, you can always try for the second row by getting behind the Pyramid, leaping down—which you'll do to collect the string of Coins floating there—and shooting to the left at the Coins.

Upon reaching the Tower at the end of the level, use the Elevators to get into the door at top. (Note: you can stand directly underneath the Elevators at the end of many levels and jump *up* onto them, instead of leaping from the sides. The advantage to this is that you can position yourself so that you'll be at the very edge of the Elevator when you leap on, already facing toward the right. If you have to waste time positioning yourself *after* you're on the Elevator, your fine-tuning may cause you to miss your ideal jump-off time.) Entering the Tower on top, you'll access a bonus stage: there, you must press the A button as if the controller were a slot machine. If your timing is right, you'll win a good many extra lives! If you enter the Tower's bottom door, you get diddly! Because of that fact, if time threatens to run out when you're near the very end of a level, it's better to *let* it do so than to compromise and go in the bottom. At worst, you'll gain back the life you lost by going in the top door. At best, you'll add two lives to your storehouse of Marios! (Three, minus the one you sacrificed.)

1/2: When you come to the first three Blocks, get the ? last if you're not Super Mario: inside is a power-up which you'll have to chase as it falls to the level below. While you're on the next platform, be aware that the Chibibo isn't bound to its platform to the right: it can come down and get you. Your next foes will be a pair of Bunbuns: Spear-dropping Flies. You can leap on top of these to kill them, or you can simply wait until each drops a Spear and then dash under it. There's plenty of time to do so. The next ? is a Coin, after which you'll cross five platforms. (Watch it—there's a pair of Nokobons here, so hit them with Super Balls or pound on them and scurry before their Bombs go off.)

After dispatching a Chibibo, you'll reach a row of Blocks with a Coin in the center—and a Nokobon on top: butt the Block and it'll fall off. Look down, to the right, and you'll see a ?. Jump down, but shift Mario so that he lands to the *left* of this. Then, carefully, move to the far left of the platform—don't move *too* far left, though, or you'll drop off the side —and leap up. There's an Invisible Block here. Hit it and you'll release a one-up. Catch it, get the Coin from the ?, then jump up on the ? Block to get to the platform to the right. There are a pair of Elevators: when you leap from the Elevator on the right, do so when it's quite high. That way, you can gather the loose change hanging in the air on your way down.

More Bunbuns attack moments later: two in the air, a third high in the air, a fourth flying very low. You can jump on the first, second, and fourth; to kill the third, rebound a Super Ball off the ground. At the Pyramid watch for the two Chibibos coming down, then climb to the top and get the ?, a power-up. (You'll have to scoot to the right, to the lowest Ledge on that side, to catch it. Just make sure you don't scoot *off* the edge of the Pyramid!) There's a trio of Elevators to the right: take them fast and you'll be in good position to get the Coins to the right—that is, a rapid crossing will place you on the third Elevator while it's high. Immediately go to the far right of the Ledge you're on, so that you're standing just under the Ledge with the Nokobon— don't worry, the Bomb-toting turtle won't come down at you. Another Bunbun will attack, but you'll be safe from its Spears here. When the flying fiend leaves, jump up, either killing or avoiding the Nokobon. The next row of Blocks contains a Coin, a one-up, and a Coin, in that order. There's a Coin in the ? below, but no Invisible Block this time.

At the next Elevator—there's just one, this time —jump to the right in such a way that you can gather the three horizontal Coins on your way to the Ledge. Two Bunbuns attack in tandem: stand as if the last tree on the right were passing through you, and their shafts won't touch you. Fire to the *right* as each one is leaving: your projectile will ricochet to the left and kill them. When you reach the final Elevator, just before the Tower, once again go for the top door and the bonus stage. There are two Blocks hanging in the air to the right of the Elevator, and you must use these as stepping-stones to get into the Tower. Thing is, you've got to get on and off them super-fast: they fall apart in less than a second. You won't die if you drop, but you won't be able to get into the top door. Don't lose heart if one of the fragile Blocks falls: you can still get in with just a single Block. The trick is to stand on the very edge of the Elevator and jump as soon as it's lined up with the word "Battery" on the left side of the Game Boy.

1/3: Whatever you do on this level, don't lose your power-up ability. Much of the treasure here requires Block-bashing ability. To begin with, go *left* so that you're standing just to the right of the wall there! Jump up and you'll uncover a secret Elevator above your head! When you do so, clear out the Coins from the ?'s on the right—taking care not to scroll the Elevator off the left side—then go back to the Block on the left side of the row, get on top of it, jump left to the Elevator, and ride it to a secret cache of Coins—28 beauties in all! You'll miss out on the wonderful things below, like Falling Rocks and Pakkun Flowers, but try not to be disappointed!

When you reach the edge of the upper Ledge, look down. Wait until the Pakkun Flower retreats into the Pipe below you, then jump in. (This Pakkun stays down for a long time, so there's no need to hurry). Once inside, go to the middle level, smash the Blocks above, go down, break the Blocks below that, then drop to the floor and bust up the Blocks there. You'll get the points *and* be able to cross the gaps and collect the Coins by pressing down the B button. Note: the second breakable Block from the right, on the bottom, contains many Coins. Just keep hitting it!

Leap the Pit when you emerge, and you'll come to four Pipes. The first two don't contain Pakkuns, but the second two do. Get on the second Pipe, wait until the Pakkun Flower goes down on the third, leap onto it, then vault over the fourth Pipe entirely. There are Coins in the row of ? Blocks you'll encounter overhead, but watch out: stop under the first ? on the left and then *immediately* back away to the left. Falling Rocks will drop just beyond that. Stand still till they stop, then get the Coins. There are more Coins in the next row of Blocks overhead, but they won't be as easy to get since a Gao is guarding them. If you have Super Balls, run ahead, stand beneath the left torch, just to the right of it, fire, run back to the left. The Ball will ricochet and eventually hit the Gao. If you *don't* have Super Balls, wait until the monster fires, then hurry onto the row of Blocks and jump down on the creature. Watch out, though: Gao can shoot up as well as down, so don't think you're immune just because you're above the creature! In either case, crack the Blocks and bop the ?'s when the menace is ended. When you're finished, go *back* to the empty space where you destroyed the Block on the right—the space to the left of the ? on the far right. Hit up again, at the empty space. Another invisible Elevator will appear! Hop on, and it will lift you to a Pipe on top where there is a very well-stocked Coin room! After collecting the Coins on the bottom, break the Blocks immediately overhead and gather 24 Coins in there. To reach the ones on top, you'll need to fire a Super Ball. Climb on the exit Pipe to get the foursome above it, then leave.

There's nothing in the small Pyramid that follows. When you get over it, hop onto the lowest tier, which contains Coins. If you're Super Mario, jump up, shattering the Blocks overhead, and get the Coins from the ?'s. (Don't worry: the Nokobon can't leave its Ledge.) When that's done, hop up and use a Super Ball against the Turtle, then get the Coins on that tier. If you have the time, press down on the controller so that Mario is squatting, then press A repeatedly so he can shimmy down the tunnel, collecting Coins. If you are running *out* of time, just stay on the Ledge where you killed the Nokobon, go right, leap over the wall, turn, squat and fire a Super Ball left down the middle walkway to collect the Coins. Stand. See the right angle formed by the Blocks above you, with the vertex in the upper left corner? Jump up into this corner and an Invisible Block will appear. Hit it repeatedly for Coins. Head

right, over the Pyramid, after pausing to make sure
the Falling Blocks there have already fallen!

Now, then—remember, above, where we said, "If
you're Super Mario . . ."? If you're *not,* all is not
lost! Instead of busting the wall, fighting the
Nokobon, and so forth, just squat and go right along
the lowest passageway. This gives you access to the
Pyramid laden with Coins. Just don't go rushing in,
though: those Falling Rocks mentioned in the last
paragraph will welcome you as you enter the treasure chamber! There's also a power-up in here.
When you reach the other side of the Pyramid, shatter the Blocks to get out. You'll come to a pair of
Sphinxes beneath a double row of Blocks: smash
them all and acquire a power-up. Leap the Bridge
that lies just beyond it, or you'll plunge to oblivion.

As soon as you get to the other side, stop: a Gao is
lurking on the far right, spitting Fireballs, though
they can't get you if you stand where you are. Just
wait until it's fired one, then charge! You'll be able
to pounce on it before it gets off another shot. Immediately after fighting one more Gao, you'll face King
Totomesu, the boss of the level. It'll take five Super
Balls to kill him: straddle the fourth and fifth
Blocks from the left, leap his first Fireball, and
shoot on the way down. If you haven't Super Balls,
you must leap over the creature: as soon as the music changes, run to the right as fast as you can.
Jump its first Fireball, then run under its second.
There's a brief interval before the next two-Fireball
sequence: run *right up to its nose* and jump over the
boss . . . making sure, when you do, that you clear
the creature's tail. You're trying to land in the
small space behind it, not on the monster itself.
(And don't try to kill the beast by landing on its
head, as you can do with lesser Gaos: you'll die.)
Once you leap the monster, it'll explode. (Another

option: if you're Super Mario but have no Super
Balls, you can run right *through* the monster. You'll
lose your power-up, but if time is running out, it *is* a
viable choice!) Step up to the stone barrier behind
the creature, and the wall will come down. You'll
enter a chamber where Daisy will appear . . . but
only to tantalize you! She'll turn into a Fly and vanish after a moment, and you'll have to proceed
to . . .

2/1: There are Coins in the ?'s in the first row of
Blocks. After that, jump down along the right wall
of the plateau on which you're standing. Notice
where the Honen is leaping from the water, then
stand on top of that spot. It will perish when it hits
the bottom of your feet. Hop up two plateaus and
dispatch the next Honen in this fashion, collect the
Coins above, then hop back to the left, down two
plateaus. Now jump onto the bottom plateau to the
right and stand on the left side. Jump up and you'll
uncover an Invisible Block with a power-up. Leap
onto the Block and pluck the Flower. If it's a Super
Mushroom, you can't catch it while standing anywhere on that Ledge: you're going to have to nab it
while leaping to the Ledge to the right. Otherwise,
it'll fall in the water.

Continue to the right. After crossing the two Elevators, get the power-up from the ? to the right of
the Pipe, shoot Super Balls to get the Coins to the
right, then drop down the Pipe. Once inside, step
onto the platform on the floor, just to your right. Hit
the uppermost block that is *attached to the wall to
your immediate right.* You'll get a power-up. Don't
pluck it . . . yet. Go to the left of the platform, hop
onto the row of two Blocks and, from there, jump up
onto the single Block above. Leap up and smash the
Block that leads into the upper cache. (Note: if you

accidentally break one of the stepping-stones while leaping up, that's not good . . . but it isn't necessarily disastrous if you have Super Ball power. Crack the Block that leads to the upstairs section anyway, go to the bottom section, and we'll tell you what to do in a moment.) Jump up and collect all but the rightmost row of Coins up here. Go to the wall on the right, carefully snatching or Super Balling the top two Coins—leaving the two below it untouched—then leave this area. Obliterate all the breakable Blocks on the left side, then go to the bottom section and gather the Coins there. When you're finished, get on top of the exit Pipe, leap up to obtain the two remaining Coins, and leave. If you were unable to get into the Coin room above, *don't* leave until you've turned left on top of the exit Pipe, squatted, and fired a Super Ball. It will ricochet into the room and clean out all but one or two of the Coins.

Outside, you'll collect Coins on several plateaus, then come to a series of Bridges with Coins along the top. You can avoid the Honen using a stop-and-go technique, or you can watch where they emerge and stand on top of them as before, killing them when they pop up. At the end of the first Bridge, wait until the Nobokon comes along on the second. Jump up and Super Ball it. If you don't have Super Ball power, wait until it turns and is headed right before proceeding. If you leap on it and kill it right away, you may run into a Honen leaping right beside it while fleeing the turtle's Bomb.

As you continue ahead, deal with the Honen as described above. Keep an eye out for the pair of Chibibos that arrive in tandem. If you jump on the first, be sure you jump again *immediately* on the second, or it'll run into you and kill you. Don't simply leap ahead to avoid them. Even though they'll wander to the left and drop off the Ledge like little lemmings, you may jump right into the Honen rising and falling on the right! In the row of Blocks to the right, you'll find a Coin in the left and a Star in the right. You'll have to leap to the right to catch the latter as it emerges. Be careful: a Chibibo has wandered onto the plateau below, so make sure you land on its head as you fall.

Run quickly while you're invincible, and you'll be able to get past the fire-breathing Yurarin: it'll attack right after the fourth plateau beyond the floating Coins. This creature turns to fire at you once you pass, so don't pause to take a breath just because you got around it! (Whether you caught the Star or not, it's a good idea to make the Pipe your goal: as soon as you've made it by the Yurarin, take a big leap over the Pipe and press yourself against the Pipe's right side. The Yurarin's Fireball won't get you there.)

The next Pipe is another Coin room. Before entering, go to the ? on the top right: multiple Coins can be found here. When you do enter the Pipe, you might be inclined to panic: after clearing the Coins off the floor, you'll notice that there doesn't seem to be any way out! Fear not. Go to the bottom right corner and jump up. This will reveal an Invisible Block that will enable you to leap up to the Coins *and* get out. Use the B button technique described earlier to cross the gaps in the walkways. However, on the lower walkway, stop before you reach the last gap or you *will* fall through it. You won't perish, but you'll waste time getting back up there. Note that you can smash the Blocks directly below the Pipe exit above.

Upon emerging, again, use repeated hits to get the Coins from the ? Block above, gather the floating Coins to the right, and pluck a Coin and power-up from the left and right, respectively, of the row of Blocks above. Immediately after this row, you'll face a Yurarin. Jump its Fireballs and position yourself on the Bridge so that the killer will come up under your feet and die. If you don't, you've got a problem: a second Yurarin pops up to the right, and if the other one is still on your left, you'll be caught in a dangerous crossfire. If this happens, leap their Fireballs while edging to the right. (Do this even if you've killed the first Yurarin . . . though facing one is obviously a whole lot easier!) Wait until it's fired, then run to the right and jump over it, onto the Ledge to the left of the Elevator. If you time your jump right, you'll have the unparalleled satisfaction of actually grazing the Yurarin's head on your way over, killing it . . . a neat bonus. Once the Yurarin is off the screen, it'll no longer fire at you. Get on the Elevator, stand on the left side, and as the Elevator is rising, bust the Block and the ? Block above: in it is a one-up. You'll have to break them both *and* jump to the Coin Ledge on the right before the Elevator descends: the one-up falls onto the Ledge and keeps rolling; if you don't get to the Ledge immediately, the one-up will fall away. Get the one-up and Coins both, then leap onto the top of the wall to the right and take a hefty jump onto the Elevator. (Note: if you're not Super Mario you can't get the one-up because you can't break the Block underneath it. Sorry.) Make a quick leap onto the platform by the Tower door and enter on top.

2/2: Your first foe here is a Mekabon, which detaches its head and sends it soaring down at you. Luckily, it isn't a homing head. As soon as you start the round, rush right, get on the Ledge, and jump on the Head before it comes off. If you fail at this, you can either attack the Head and body separately, or simply stay out of the Head's way. When it reattaches itself to the body, leap up and come down on top of it. So long Mekabon. Use the B button to run across the string of Blocks and gaps to the right. There's a power-up in the first Block: it'll drift to the right, and you'll have to jump to catch it. Make sure that when you do, you land on top of the wall *or* on the Chibibo waiting for you. You'll find a Coin in the second ?. Before you can crawl down the Pipe, it will be necessary to kill the Nokobon on top. Jump onto the Block to the left of the Pipe, and either fire at or hop on the turtle to kill it. If you did the latter, quickly leap back to the Block on the left or onto either side of the platform on which the Pipe is resting, to avoid the Bomb. When it detonates, get on the Pipe, hop up to grab the Coins above, then drop down.

In the Pipe, the uppermost Block on the wall immediately to your right contains multiple Coins. As you did in the 2/1 treasure room of this design, take care not to shatter any Blocks. Follow the same procedure here as you did there. Leaving the Pipe, get the Coin in the ? to the left (again), then collect the Coins above and head right. There's a Coin in the next two ?'s, and then a pair of Elevators: climb onto the ? you last hit to board the horizontal transports. However, be alert: when you leap off the second (last) Elevator, jump high so you can sweep up the vertical line of Coins to the right. As you fall, shift to the left so you land on the Pipe and not on the Nokobon to its right. If you land on the creature, get onto the Pipe *fast* or you'll blow up!

If you're not Super Mario and you don't want to face the robot to the right, just hop to the stone Ledge on the right, then step off to the left: an invisible walkway extends slightly over the water. Proceed on the lower level. Harvest all the Coins here, facing only minimal opposition from a trio of Chibibos. Deal with these by staying to the left side of any tunnel in which they appear, just to the left of the Column: that's the only area where there's room enough for you to jump. Wait for them to return to the left before making a leap onto their noggins. (Note: if you choose to go across the top, stand on the Ledge to the upper right of the Pipe, wait until the Mekabon's head reattaches, then leap up and attack it. Up here, you won't get nearly as many Coins, but you *will* find a Star in the last Block on the right of the first overhead row. Cross on top, kill the Mekabon below you at the other end, then jump down and get the Star.) Your relatively safe passage ends when you come to a Nokobon waiting for you on the other side. Wait until it starts walking right, then jump over. A Chibibo will attack; leap on it, then kill the Nokobon and dodge the Fireballs of one of your old friends, a Yurarin, who's rising and falling on the right. Using the Blocks on the ground to shield you from the flame-spitter, leap when the monster goes down, timing the jump to hit its head when he rises—otherwise, you'll have it breathing flame at your back while you deal with the Mekabon that arrives on the right.

After crowning the robot—head and body both, remember, or it'll regenerate—you'll come to a pair of Elevators, the first one moving vertically, the second horizontally. When you reach the row of Blocks with a single Block above it, hit them all for Coins. Mind you, the Nokobon and Yurarin to the right may have something to say about that: so, when you leave the Elevator, jump onto the Ledge as the Nokobon is walking to the right. Walk with it. When it turns left, you turn left as well: when you clear the leftmost ?, jump up, land on the turtle,

then run to the right under the row of ?'s to avoid
the blast. Clear out the ?'s, then, between Fireballs
from the Yurarin, climb up and get the Coin from
the ? on top. Jump down onto the big Block to the
right—the Fireballs can't touch you here—then
time your jump to kill the Yurarin as you leap to
the Block on the right. If you fail at this, hurry and
get behind the Block to the right of the Pipe, where
you'll be safe. Kill the Chibibo below you, get the
Coin from the ?, then wait until the Pakkun Flower
in the Pipe to the right sinks away. When it does,
hop on, get the Coins above, and slide into the Pipe.
Clean the Coins from the bottom, then stand just to
the left of the leftmost Block of the second row.
Jump up to uncover the Invisible Block here, and
ascend. Make sure you butt the left block under the
exit Pipe before leaving: there are multiple Coins
here.

Exit, get the Coin in the ? to the left, grab the
Coins above, and hop on the Blocks to go right. Hit
the ? for a Coin, then climb onto that Block and try
and hop to the Elevator which shifts from side to
side. (Miracles happen!) This leads to the top door.
More than likely, you'll have to take the Block
staircase. Be *real* quick about it: each Block col-
lapses the instant you step on it! There is no bonus
stage at the end of this round.

2/3: This level is all water and it scrolls *by itself*—
you just go along with the flow. Stay mostly toward
the left of the screen, darting ahead to sweep up the
Coins, then getting back. If you're Super Mario,
look for existing gaps in walls: that's less you'll
have to shoot in order to fit through. Blast Yurarins
the *instant* they appear: their Fireballs are deadly,
even underwater. Torion will not only come at you
from the right, they'll turn if you haven't shot

them, and come at you again from the left—though only once. Don't shoot or touch the Gunions: they won't bother you if you don't bother them. Touch them and you die; hit them with projectiles, and they split in two and attack. Also, if you get to the left of a Block and you get scrolled into the left side of the screen, you'll perish.

Pay attention to your surroundings, there are items to collect: a power-up in the first collection of Blocks on top, and, perhaps most importantly, a Star in the second set of Blocks on the bottom. Just make sure you're quick once you uncover it. Being so close to the bottom of the water, the Star is swallowed up quickly by the sands. When you obtain invincibility, hurry to the far right, shooting ahead. (Remember: you're impervious as long as the song runs!) When the last bars of music sound, return to the left. Upon reaching the first Column that has a narrow channel in the bottom, blast the lower four Blocks to get a power-up. You can really rack up the Coins when you come to the region where they spell MARIO—just sweep up and down on the left; no enemy will bother you here. And blast just below the midsection of the Column ahead for a Heart. (If you want a big advantage here, do something to kill yourself after you get the one-up. You'll come back to life *before* the MARIO coin section and will be able to add as many lives as you want to your collection!) Watch for the last (fourth) Column in this series of Columns: the top section contains a power-up. (Note: on this level, if you're Mario and you run up against a wall of Blocks, you need only clear out one tier to get through. Super Mario requires two. That *can* be a handicap if you're busy fending off fish. Also note: any projectiles fired by creatures, such as Yurarin, do *not* disintegrate when the monster dies. Keep an eye on these while you're battling the source! These can be especially dangerous while you're passing through channels in the Blocks: if they enter the other side while you're inside, you're cooked!)

You'll be battling Tamao and Dragonzamasu at the end of this realm. Tamao is a blob that cannot be destroyed. Thus, all you can do is avoid it. While so doing, you must also fire at its boss behind it. Dragonzamasu spits Fireballs which have to be dodged while you shoot at the creature. It takes 20 hits to destroy Dragonzamasu . . . though, fortunately, it isn't necessary to slay it. When Dragonzamasu rises, get behind the block in front of it—you can use this Block for protection from the boss's fire when he's down; it can't hit you here, though Tamao can. Shoot the three Blocks of the bottom row to the right. Dart into the narrow tunnel you've created. When Dragonzamasu rises again, slide to the left and rise slightly, knock out the three Blocks on the row above it, and pilot your ship on into the opening to win the round.

3/1: When the Batadon arrives—which it does, instantly—shift to the left. It will fly in that direction, at which point you must run to the right, jump on the Pipe, get the Coin, and leap over the Pit . . . all before the Batadon flies right. There's a Nokobon at the second Pipe, but that won't present a problem. There are two row of Blocks, and a power-up in the rightmost Block on the top. Get it, then leap quickly across the Bridge that follows, since it will collapse beneath you. Land on the Nokobon on the other side, then watch out when leaping onto the Pipe to get the Coin in the Block on the right: a Cannon that fires Gira is in the next Pipe to the right. You can step on the projectile to stop it . . . but, frankly, it's less risky to avoid it altogether. Just time your progress so that you can get on top of the Cannon Pipe when the Cannon is submerged. (Note: you can stand on a Pipe when the Cannon comes up, and rise on top of it. You can also stand to one side or the other on the Pipe and not be hurt when a Gira is launched. What you *can't* do is try to get up while the Cannon is firing!) Slip down the Pipe, getting the Coins by leaping over the Spikes *carefully*.

When you emerge, get to the ? on the top right: there are multiple Coins in here. Unfortunately, a Batadon guards it. When the creature is to the right —and this strategy goes for all the Batadons you'll face on this level—leap onto the Z-shaped Ledge to the left, above you. (You can't hide under that Ledge: it'll get you there, even though it looks as though the creature can't fit!) Step on the Batadon's head when it comes after you. (Note: if the Batadon kills you, take heart in the fact that it won't be there when you go to your next Mario.) You can get up to 17 Coins from the Block above! You'll have to kill the Nokobon to the Ledge on the right in order to get to the Elevators. Upon reaching them, note that the middle one is extremely narrow, so don't jump with your usual abandon. You'll find a Pak- kun Flower in the next Pipe, and a Nokobon on the Column to its right. This is tricky: if you don't have Super Balls, you must to hop from the Elevator onto the turtle, then *immediately* jump onto the Column to its right *or* back to the Pipe—if the Pakkun is submerged—to avoid the explosion. In either case, leap onto the turtle *only* when it's on the left side of the Column, or you'll perish. Use Super Balls, if you have them, to reap the Coins floating between the Columns as you jump overhead.

After the Columns, you'll find a Pakkun Flower in the first Pipe and a Cannon in the second. Hop

over the first, wait until the Cannon goes down,
then jump onto the Cannon Pipe and continue on
your way, making sure you collect the Coins from
the Blocks overhead. Be prepared to face your first
Tokotoko: the wonderfully animated stone head
runs at you, rattling its fist. You can stop it by jumping onto its head or simply leaping it and letting it
run past. A second Tokotoko will drop down at you
from the Ledge to the left of the vertical column of
floating Coins. As soon as it does so, another
Batadon will attack. Bop the Tokotoko before the
winged creature arrives, then deal with it as you did
the first one you faced—the landscape is virtually
identical. Collect the column of Coins, then climb
the Blocks to the right, drop down, and jump up to
get a Coin from the ?. You'll be standing on another
Z-shaped Ledge. Climb down to the Ledge on the
right, jump up, and you'll uncover an Invisible
Block with a Heart. You'll have to leap the Pit to
the right to catch it . . . and when you do, it's important that you drop down through the gap to the
Ledge below as *fast as possible,* since a very dogged
Batadon will show up within moments. Go back to
the Z-shaped Ledge and kill it as you did before.
(Here's an alternate plan you can try: before hitting
the Invisible Block, step onto the Ledge to the right
of the Z-shaped Ledge and go to the right edge.
That'll bring on the Batadon. Carefully walk back
to the left and *step* up onto the Z-shaped Ledge.
Don't jump back up onto that Ledge, or you'll bump
into the Invisible Block and uncover the Heart; with
the Batadon there, you'll never be able to get it. Kill
the Batadon as before, and then uncover the Heart.)
   Upon the creature's demise, climb to the right,
stomp the Nokobon, collect the floating Coins in the
vertical Column, then jump down onto the verti-
cally-shifting Elevator. Transfer to the horizontal

one, mindful of the fact that there's a Cannon in the Pipe beyond and one in the Pipe beyond that . . . so you'll have two of them firing at you while you're still on the Elevator! Leap onto the Giras as they pass to destroy them, or simply hop over them, then jump on the first Pipe when the Cannon goes down. Hit the Block above for a power-up, then leap onto the second Pipe when the Cannon's down and *be on your toes!* Jump off and *rush* ahead to the Ledge beyond, the one on which the Pipe is sitting—it's a row of Blocks comprised of ?'s. A trio of Tokotokos comes rushing along, only *these* heads turn once they reach the left side of the screen and attack again! If you're on the left side of the Ledge, you can jump down and bop them. If you're *really* good, you can actually graze the heads of at least two of the Tokotokos as you leap onto the Ledge, killing them. Once the running heads are defeated, leap immediately onto the Coin Ledge to the left so that you can be above the Batadon when it arrives. You'll be able to leap down on it, then go under the Pipe Ledge, bash the ?'s, and collect the Coins—taking care not to get hit by the Cannon in the *next* Pipe, and also keeping an eye out for the two Batadons and more Tokotokos which attack.

Surviving these, you face an even tougher challenge: Ganchan riding. The Ganchan are boulders that come rolling at you from the right. They'll kill you if you let them . . . but they're also your ticket over the Spike fields that follow. (Note: the instructions refer to the Spikes as "Needles." Sorry, but somebody needs glasses! Those deadly shafts are fat and tapered; something must have gotten lost in the translation from Japanese.) Go to the edge of the Block wall where the Spike fields begin. Stand facing right, with Mario's foot *over* the edge of the wall, on thin air. When the rock comes along, it will go

under your foot, pick you up, and carry you through
the air. As soon as you reach a wall of Blocks, however, make sure you get off or you'll perish. (If you
fall on Spikes as Super Mario, hop off quickly and
you'll survive.) Position yourself on that wall as you
did on the previous one, with a foot over the side,
and hitch a ride on the next Ganchan. Repeat until
you come to a Ledge shaped like an inverted L in
the air. Get on the left (lower) side of the Ledge and
wait until the Ganchan has come down. If you stand
on the right side, this rock won't give you a lift: it'll
kill you! As soon as the boulder has rolled down at
the Ledge, leap to the right, *on top* of the object.
Ride it to the wall and get off before it sinks down
into a Pit. Leap the Spikes to the fat, horizontal
Ledge laden with Coins. When you've cleared these
away, leap onto one of the Ganchan materializing
on the upper right. Ride it to the Elevator, and hop
from this into the top of the Tower. If you missed
that Coin Ledge, don't worry: you can proceed along
the bottom. Just hop from the small outcrops, over
the Spikes, to the Tower at the end. These leaps are
relatively easy to make . . . provided you start *at
once.* Those Ganchans that materialize at the right
begin bouncing in your direction. Nor do they disappear. They'll keep rolling left and right where you
have to jump, making your passage difficult, to say
the least! However: let *one* appear. Allow it to roll
after you until you reach the Tower. Then hop on
top of it, ride it to the Elevator, and leap up into the
bonus room.

3/2: In the early going, the most dangerous foe
you'll face are the Suu: spiders resembling the
Stalactites in which they hide, making them tough
to spot while you're looking out for other foes! Still,
they're easy enough to avoid if spotted: if you inch

forward, you'll trigger the arachnid's descent. All
you need do, then, is quickly back up a bit, wait
until the Suu goes up again—as Hemingway said,
"The Suu Always Rises"—then rush ahead.

The first Suu falls after the third Pipe. (There's
nothing in these Pipes, so don't bother checking.)
After you pass it, you'll face a Nokobon. Bop it and
clear the ?'s overhead: all contain Coins. There's another Suu and Nokobon ahead—easily dealt with—
followed by a Pipe with a pair of Suus beyond it.
"Trigger" the Suu on the left by getting onto the
Pipe and dropping down to its right—but not *so* far
right that you're under the Suu! When the spider on
the left has started up, run ahead; you'll clear the
second Suu before it drops. (If you want to kill them,
wait until they're down and then jump on their
backs.) There's a Pakkun Flower in the next Pipe:
when the plant retreats, get on the Pipe and stand
there until the Suu beyond it has come down. Leap
onto the Block in the waterfall, and from there onto
the Coin Ledge. Sweep up the money and stop on
the right side of the Ledge: a different kind of spider, a Kumo, makes its debut here, hopping along
like the Flies of 1/1. As soon as it's below the Ledge,
fall onto its back, killing the creature.

Hop onto the Column to the right to trigger the
Suu, then proceed to the next Coin Ledge . . .
watching out for the Suu overhead. Get below the
Ledge and hit the last Block on the right for a
power-up. Continuing to the right, you'll find a Coin
in the Block overhead. Cross the Waterfall by hopping the Blocks, then *quickly* dispose of the
Nokobon on the Ledge. A Kumo will arrive almost
at once, and if you have to deal with it and the
Nokobon, you'll have your hands (and feet) full.
This Kumo will attack you on the Ledge where
you're standing, so be ready to leap up and land on

top of it. When you've killed the beasts and cleared away the Coins, get beneath the Ledge. Break the Blocks as you did back in 1/3 to reveal a hidden Elevator. Ride it to the top and jump *left*—using the A button; don't try walking on air with the B button or you'll fall. Enter the Pipe and collect the 100 Coins therein. There's also a power-up in the ?, which you may need to break Blocks in this treasure room. When you leave the Pipe, gather the Coins to the left, then drop off the Ledge.

When you continue to the right, it'll be necessary to leap onto a thin Column. If that weren't difficult enough, you have to get off it *immediately:* a Stalactite will fall, killing you if you linger more than a moment. (When you jump onto the Column, make sure that the Nokobon on the Ledge beyond is headed to the right. Otherwise, you'll hop onto the Column and then to the Ledge, where you'll land on the Bomb-bearing sucker!) After killing the Nokobon, you'll have to get past a pair of Suu. Wait until the first one comes down, then leap on its back. You can't wait until it rises and then jump: the arc of your leap will carry you right into the creature's furry legs. Run over the second Suu as well, kill the Nokobon on the Ledge, wait there for the Kumo to arrive, jump on it, then leap to the right, clear the Coins from the Ledge, cross the Waterfall, and get the power-up from the single overhead Block . . . watching out for the Gira being launched by the Cannon in the Pipe to the right. Hop the Cannon—or get on top of it and then leap to the other side—and hug the right side of the Pipe: there's a Suu overhead, waiting to drop. When it retreats, clear the Coins from the Blocks overhead.

After crossing the Waterfall, you'll encounter a Kumo on the first Ledge. Be on your guard so you land on it! (Incidentally, you'll find with this and most previous Kumos that if you position yourself beneath the "tens" numeral of your Coin counter, you'll be in an ideal position to jump onto the creature.) Cross the other Ledges (no problem!) and you'll find yourself at a Spike Pit—keep an eye out for a Block with multiple Coins here. Ride the Ganchan across . . . only on this level, you have to leap onto the boulder to get aboard. To time your leap right, wait until the rock has hit the Spikes and has just begun it's ascent toward the left before jumping. Get off, leap onto the next Ganchan to cross another Spike Pit, then watch out: there's a world of trouble awaiting you on the other side. You'll face a Cannon in the next Pipe, a Kumo on the other side, and a Suu above. But all is not as bleak as it seems: when you leave the rock, hug the left side of the Pipe. Get on top of the Cannon—that will trigger the Suu—leap the ugly arachnid when it descends (and when the Kumo is on the right), then crush the Kumo when you come down. A snap! If you opt to go down that Pipe, you'll find a multiple-Coin Block near the center of the treasure room. Also: if you don't want to go Spike-hopping, you can access the lower row of Coins by getting at them from below. Even if you're not Super Mario, you can hit these Blocks and get the bottom row of Coins. Ride the Elevators to the right—taking care not to die when bopping the Nokobon on the Ledge between them *and* making sure you jump from the left Elevator when it's low or you'll expire when you hit the Stalactites above—and you'll come to those same fragile Blocks you've had to deal with at the end of the last few levels . . . except that if you fail to cross *these,* you won't just lose out on the top room of a Tower. You'll perish! The trick here is *not* to step on each one. There are two Blocks, then a solid Ledge, then another two more Blocks. Leap on the second one from the left, quickly hop to the solid Ledge, then jump *not* onto the next Block, but onto the one beyond it. Leap off at once. If any of the Blocks after this one collapse before you can get off them, you'll land on solid ground below, which leads directly to the Tower. You won't get to the top room . . . but you won't perish either!

3/3: After you pass a Pipe and two Columns, you're going to face five tricky Elevators: the first, third, and fifth slide from side to side; the second and fourth shift diagonally to the upper right and left, respectively. To cross: when you reach the first Column, do *not* jump at once onto the first Elevator. Wait until it comes back a second time. In quick succession go from it to the second to the third, then stop. Wait until the fourth comes near, then go to it and then onto the last one rapidly. When you hop from the last one, watch out: a Ganchan comes rolling along. Jump over it. Collect the Coins from atop the Pipe, cross a Column, and get onto the Elevator. Do *not* jump onto the Column to the right. Rather, ride the Elevator up and jump quickly onto and off of the collapsible Blocks and over to the Pipe. Just make sure you time your move so that you land on the Pipe when the Pakkun Flower is down. Inside is a power-up and 100 Coins.

Upon leaving the Pipe, hop onto the second Column to the right and jump up: there's an Invisible Block with a power-up here. Get onto the rightmost Column and leap onto the Kumo. Get back on the little wall to the left: another Kumo will arrive. Stand there and simply drop down on it. Go to the Ledge above to collect not just the Coins, but a one-up in the fourth block from the right. Six Elevators await: the first moves from side to side, the second to the upper right, the third to the upper left, the fourth vertically, and the fifth and sixth horizontally. You can actually avoid the sixth if you wish, but there are Coins you can only access from that Elevator—and every one is precious at this level. Immediately after the Elevators is a Pipe. There are Coins, as well as multiple Coins in the bottom Block on the center. Just be careful not to fall on the Spikes!

When you emerge, you can reach the Ledges above by uncovering an Invisible Block to the right of the Pipe. Hop the Ledges to the next Pipe, where it will be necessary to board the horizontal Elevator below. Make certain that you do so while it's moving to the right, or you'll die. Hop up from the Elevator when it passes below and to the right of the Ledge overhead. Jump from that Ledge to the top Ledge on the right, then down onto the Elevator when it's shifting to the right. Jump from the Elevator to the Ledge on the right, then up to the Ledge on the left, then to the top Ledge. Fall and go right. When you reach the "altar" of Blocks, a Batadon will arrive: leap onto the altar when the flying monster goes left, then jump down onto it. A Tokotoko is waiting on the other side but won't present much difficulty. Vault onto the next altar and get a power-up from the leftmost ? and Coins from the two on the right. Just don't get flattened by the Ganchan, which comes rolling down from the steps on the right. Leap the Pit and clear the Coins from the next row—this time, watching out for a Batadon. All you have to do is get on top of the ? row and jump down on the monster, then clear out the Coins. Climb the next set of steps and leap the Waterfall. Once you're across, it's time to tango with Hiyoihoi—a Tokotoko who flings Ganchans at you. If you're not Super Mario, you've got virtually no

chance of getting past the monster. Though there's
a Ledge above Hiyoihoi, you can hitch a ride on
Ganchan after Ganchan, edging closer each time,
and then leap up. (Fortunately, if you die here, you
go back to where the power-up was located!) The
way to get through is leap the boulders and shoot
the albino with ten Super Balls. If you're Super Mario *and* desperate, you can waste your power-up by
taking a hit from a boulder as you literally run
through Hiyoihoi.

4/1: Bop the three ?'s for Coins, then go left and go
down the Pipe, skewing right as you do so or you'll
miss the Coin Ledge. If you stay above ground: get
the Coins in the first three ?'s and a power-up in the
Block on the left of the next row. The second inverted Pipe contains a Pakkun Flower nipping
down at you; the upward-opening Pipe after it also
contains a Pakkun. If you don't have Super Balls,
move past the first when it withdraws, wait until
the second Pakkun goes down, and move on.
(There's nothing in the Blocks overhead here.)
You'll find Coins in the next two Blocks, but a
Pionpi comes hopping at you from the right. These
beings can only be stunned for five seconds by leaping on them: shooting them with two Super Balls is
the one way to make sure they stay dead. If you're
unarmed, stun the little fellow and move on, hurrying past the Pakkun Flower to the next two ?'s,
which also contain Coins. Keep in mind that the
Pionpi will follow you until you board the Elevators.
  Leap off the second Elevator onto the two ?
Blocks, going down and clearing the Coins from
them between shots from the Cannon on the right.
Get onto the Cannon, hopping onto the row of ?'s
and clearing the Coins from them when the Pionpi
is headed left. When you leap the Ledge, you'll be

greeted by another Pionpi and a bomb-toting turtle: get the latter before the former arrives. The three Blocks immediately overhead contain nothing, but the sole ? on top has multiple Coins. Don't leap the Pit immediately: wait for a second Pionpi to arrive. Wait until he's gone to the left, then proceed. Why did you wait? Because the next Ledge is a duplicate of this one, except that there are *two* Nokobons to deal with. If the Pionpi hadn't come over, he would have been waiting for you there! The Blocks above you contain nothing; the single ? on top has just one Coin. Wait and, again, let a Pionpi come over from beyond the Pit to the right, so that you only have to deal with one Pionpi when you get there.

Cross the Pit to the Pipes: the third and fourth contain Pakkuns, and there's a Cannon in the fifth. Worse, the Pionpi will cross the Pit and come after you. So, hop the Pipes as soon as the Pakkuns go down, get on top of the Cannon, and jump to the last Pipe in that row—it's the tallest one; the Giras won't hit you up there. Across the Pit there's a Pakkun Flower in the second Pipe and a Pionpi just to the right of it. Hop onto the Pipe when the Pakkun goes down, kill or stun the Pionpi, scroll him off the screen by hopping onto the first Pipe—he won't return—then double back and clear the Coins from the three ?'s overhead. Hop on the Pakkun Pipe when the Flower goes down, get on the last Pipe, and leap onto the Elevator. The first Elevator moves diagonally to the upper left, the next to the upper right. They're a piece of cake. You'll come to five Pipes in a row: one opening up, two opening down, another up, and the last armed with a Cannon. The first four all contain Pakkuns, so proceed using the stop-and-go technique—making sure that after the third Pipe, you hit the last Block on the overhead

Ledge: there are multiple Coins—then jump onto the Cannon Pipe when the weapon is down.

There's a Pakkun in the next downward-opening Pipe: hurry past it when it withdraws and wait. A Chibibo will come by, and you'll want to get rid of it before continuing—taking care that you don't jump up into a Gira from the Cannon. Once the mushroomtop is slain, do stop-and-go past the Pakkuns in the Pipes: when you come to an overhead Ledge of breakable Blocks, hit the last Block for a power-up. Once again, stop-and-go past the Pakkun Pipes, the first and fourth of which open up, the middle two opening downward. The last Block on the Ledge overhead here contains multiple Coins. (Just watch out for the falling Block, like those you dealt with in 1/3.) When you've cleared the next two Elevators, you'll have to cross a series of breakable Blocks *fast* and then avoid the Cannon in the second Pipe and the Pionpi beyond. Land on the Cannon, bop the little man, and continue right, leaping the next Pionpi and defeating the two Chibibos. (There's a power-up in the lone block overhead: wait on the Chibibos if you need Super Balls, get them, then blast the little critters.) Leap onto the Elevator on the other side and jump onto the Ledge: you'll find a power-up in the Block above. A third Elevator will take you to a Ledge: jump from it to the Ledge on the right, then up to the left, to the L-shaped Coin repository above. Be careful, though, when you return to the Ledge on the right after reaping the riches: to the right are *three* Cannons firing at you from three different heights! It'll be necessary to jump from the top of one Cannon to the next, taking care not to step on the Chibibo marching sentrylike after the second Cannon. After you clear the last Cannon, three Pionpis will charge at once on the other side: shoot or bop 'em *fast*.

There's a Coin in the ? atop the row of three Blocks, and three more Cannon after that, firing at different heights, as before. The only difference is that there's no Chibibo here; deal with them as before. You'll see the Elevator to the right: before you jump onto it, note where the Cannon are firing—they'll have changed direction because you've passed them. Plan your move accordingly, going from the Elevator to the collapsible Blocks and into the room at the top of the Tower.

4/2: Begin by leaping the Ledges over the water; there's no danger until you reach the two ?'s overhead. There's a Chibibo on the Ledge beneath them. Poise yourself on the right edge of the Ledge above the Chibibo and shoot it or drop onto it. Scurry to the right before it explodes, then go back to the ?'s and collect the Coins. Repeat this procedure at the next Chibibo . . . though you'll also have to keep an eye on the Pompon Flower below. It isn't difficult to avoid . . . as long as you don't rush ahead. Wait until the Flower is on the far *left*, then do as before, with one exception. After you bop the Chibibo, *rush* to the right and hop onto the row of ?'s. The reason? A Cannon is firing from the right, and will nail you if you dally. After the Gira has passed and the Chibibo has exploded, hit the ?'s for power-ups. Leap up to the Ledge on the right and drop down on the top of the Cannon. There's a Chibibo to the right, but that doesn't matter: you're going to go down the Cannon Pipe, and the turtle will be gone when you emerge.

It's vital that you have Super Ball power in the Pipe, since there are 200 Coins in here and *no* Blocks. You can clear out half of them without Super Balls—some from the ground, others by leaping off the top of the Exit Pipe—but the weapon is a

big help. When you reach the Dragon, hop onto the
Ledge level with it, to the left, and jump up. This
will cause the monster to fire its flame up, leaving
the way clear for you to leap to the right and bop it
on the head. After the Dragon, bust the Wall with
the Chibibo behind it and collect the goodies up
there. (All Coins, save for a power-up, second Block
from the left.) If you aren't Super, you must stay
below and will find Pakkun Flowers in all the down-
facing Pipes. Go through them using stop-and-go,
but scroll the screen *slowly:* when you reach the
Wall on the right, you're going to hop up to the left
to get some of the goodies on top. When you go back
to the wall, be ready to leap down fast: a Cannon to
the right is firing at you.

You'll travel through an identical set of Pipes
with Pakkun Flowers—plus the Cannon that was
firing at you—after which you'll reach another series of Ledges: there's a Chibibo on the Ledge to the
upper right, and a Pompon Flower below it. Leap
onto the bottom/center Ledge when you can leap
over the Pompon—this is not difficult—and get the
power-up from the left Block above you. Then it's
time for some fun with a new menace: the Sparks.
These are little Fireballs that orbit Blocks in a
counterclockwise direction. (In general: for the
Sparks on the ground, it's safe to stand directly to
either side of the central Block, or on top of it. The
Spark won't touch you here, and you'll definitely
want these havens as you edge your way through.)
Hop over the first Spark, then watch out at the second one, located above: there's a Pakkun Flower in
the Pipe below it. Wait until the Flower is down and
the Spark is moving away, then leap the Pipe and
hug the right side until you can move past the third
Spark. A Chibibo is waiting beyond this one; kill it,
then approach the fourth Spark, which also has a

Chibibo patrolling under it. Wait until the turtle has moved to the right before going after it: kill it, then return to the ? that was the hub of the fourth Spark. (The Spark will be gone, having been scrolled off the screen to the left.) Bop the ? and get a Star, which should last you through the next Dragon.

After you get the Star, you'll cross a pair of horizontally-shifting Elevators, after which there's another power-up in the ? that is the hub of the first Spark on this side. There's a second Spark, and another set of horizontally-shifting Elevators; watch when you jump off the second Elevator or you'll hit your head on the overhead Block and fall in the water. Wait until the Elevator is *all the way* to the right before getting off. Also beware the Chibibo waiting for you on the other side. There's an Invisible Block with a Coin directly above the Pipe to the right of the lower Elevator. When you reach the Dragon, deal with it as you did the previous one. You'll pass two more Sparks. Kill the Chibibo on the Ledge above, get back down when it explodes—and also to avoid the Spark—continue past the second Spark, and you'll face a third Dragon. After defeating it, run across the widely spaced Blocks using the B button technique, making sure you stop after the last Block so you don't run into the Pakkun Flower in the downward-facing Pipe. When you reach the end of the platform, get to the *very edge* and jump up and slightly to the right when the vertically-moving Elevator is down. If you're not on the edge, you won't be able to get on the lift. Upon getting off at the top, you'll notice there's a breakable Block in the Bridge. Step on it and fall with it, skewing Mario to the right as you do so. If you *don't* shift him to the side, he won't land on solid ground and will perish. If you need more time to study your surround-

ings as you fall, simply hop up: even though the
Block is dropping, it's still solid. Climb to the top of
the Tower.

4/3: This level's a lot like 2/3 in terms of strategy:
like that round, this one scrolls, inexorably, and
you're borne along with the wind. The only difference is that you should play in the middle as soon as
the Rocketons start appearing: they not only fire
forward, but also backward. You'll want to give
yourself some extra maneuvering room to avoid
their missiles—which, alas, are immune to your
own blasts and also survive the scrolling-off or de-
struction of the ship.

Very few of the Blocks contain useful objects.
There are power-ups in the first and fifth Blocks
overhead, and a Star two Blocks later, overhead. Indeed, it's a good idea to play this round entirely in
the upper half until you reach the maze: there's virtually nothing of use below. It's easy enough to
shoot at the Blocks on top, since you'll be firing in
that direction to kill enemies anyway! When you
first enter the maze, hang to the left until you clear
out the four foes that attack. They can go through
Walls—you can't, of course—so beware! Enemies
will only appear in the first few corridors of the
maze. After they stop attacking, you'll enter a massive Coin room. When you've cleaned it out —you
have to do this by touching them: your bullets won't
garner them here—drop to the bottom, shoot the
lower right-hand Wall, and continue. Your course
after shattering the Wall will be right, up, right,
down, right, up, right, down, and finally right.
What's important here is that you stay to the right
and go up and down vertical corridors as quickly as
possible: the screen will scroll you left faster than
you think! Fortunately, there are no enemies in

here to distract you. When you exit, you'll have to face three Sparks: one alone, at first—simply stay on the bottom to avoid it—then two, one atop the other. You can pass the second two, as well, by staying on the bottom. However, when you roll into their domain, you'll want to go up: there's a two-Block Wall on top, and the upper Block contains a power-up. You'll definitely want that so you can take a hit and not perish in the climactic two showdowns. Get the Coins above you to the right, then watch out for the enemies lurking in the two downward-opening Pipes: a pair of massive mailed Fists. *Don't* delay going through them: if the screen scrolls too far, you'll be *forced* to the right, and not necessarily at the best time. Head forward the instant the Fists go back in the very first time.

Once you've passed these, you'll shoot through a Wall and face the evil Blokinton, boss of this level. As soon as you've gone through the Wall, stay in the upper half of the room, firing ahead; you'll get in a few licks before the Cloudlike creature attacks you. You must hit the Cloud 20 times to destroy it: the task is complicated by the vehicles that constantly emerge from the Cloud in pairs. Blast these, and stay directly in front of the puffy thug—that is, to the left—whenever you can. Go to the right of Blokinton, and above or below it, only when it heads left; if you don't, it'll pin you to the left Wall and kill you. Then, as soon as the Cloud shifts back to the right, get on the left side of it again and continue firing. When Blokinton is history, go to the lower right corner, open fire, and get set to battle Tatanga himself. The villain is nestled inside the "war robot" Pagosu, which rises from the floor and launches projectiles that divide, each piece accelerating and fanning out at you. Though these can be felled by a single shot, they keep you from hitting your main target. Stay in the upper left corner of the screen, moving up and down only slightly to avoid the projectiles while you get in your shots at the big boss. It'll take at least two dozen direct hits on Pagosu's cannons to disable the ship and release Tatanga's captive, Daisy. (And, of course, bring on the credits scroll! Speaking of which—congrats to programmers M. Yamaoto and T. Harada, and director S. Okada, for an absolutely terrific game.)

After you win, press Start and the game will begin again . . . though not exactly as you remembered it! Though all the goodies are in the same place as before, your foes have multiplied rather significantly. For example, you'll find a Fly at the first one-up in 1/1, and a Gao—yes, a Gao!—perched atop the first multiple Coin Block. Bunbuns attack right away in 1/2, there are more falling Blocks than before in 1/3 . . . and wherever there was one Gao in that level the first time around, there are now two. A pair of Tamao work with Dragonzamasu at the conclusion of 2/3—though that won't affect your strategy at all—while you'll be greeted by a Cannon in the first Pipe of 3/1 . . . and so on. Fortunately, you get continues if you lose at any level the second time around. (The continue mode actually begins in the closing levels of the first game. For instance, if you make it to Blokinton's chamber and lose your last Mario, you'll start level 4/3 again with three continues.)

Extra Tips: When you become super-proficient at *Super Mario Land,* you'll even be able to execute level select. All you have to do is make your way through the game *twice.* (Are there batteries that last that long?) After you do so, a prompt will ask you to select the round and realm you wish to visit. Make your choice with the control pad.

If you're having trouble with the game, you can earn as many lives as you wish . . . assuming you have time and patience. In level 1/1, after you collect the first Star, continue to where the three rows of Blocks give you eight Coins. When you've collected these, leap off the cliff to the right, losing a Mario. When you return, you'll be right underneath the Block where you got the Star. Repeat this process as often as you like! The Heart will keep replacing the life you lost, while those Coins keep on accumulating, giving you extra Marios. (Just don't take a power-up: Super Mario, sans Super Balls, can't get the Coins nestled in those narrow corridors of the Wall at the end of the level.)

Finally, do the following at the end of world 1/1: if you get into the top of the Tower, hold down the A button while the time-remaining is being added to your score. *Keep* the button pressed as you shift into the bonus stage. You'll be rewarded with three extra Marios almost every time.

Rating: A
A great adventure which successfully captures the wonder and thrills of the NES Super Mario Bros. Games.

TETRIS

Type: Placing odd shapes into neat piles

Object: Geometric shapes known as Tetrads are raining from above! If you can maneuver them so that one or more segments form an unbroken horizontal line, that line will disappear and any Tetrads above it will fall. If, however, the screen fills so that a part of any piece touches the top, the game ends.

Hero: There are seven kinds of Tetrads: Z-shaped facing left, Z-shaped facing right, L-shaped facing left, L-shaped facing right, T-shaped, Flat, and Square. You can rotate these so that any of its composite Blocks are pointing up, down, or sideways, and you can shift the Tetrads to the left or right. Once they touch down you have only a second to slide them under another Tetrad if you wish.

Villains: Only the mounting pile of Tetrads!

Points: Erasing lines gets you points, but the real trick is to erase four at once—aka, a Tetris. Tetris scores increase geometrically, meaning that your fifth will be worth far more than your first. In the A game, putting any Tetrad onto the pile earns points. Earn 100,000 playing the A game, and you'll get to see a rocket—looks like a Conestoga 400, in case you were wondering—blast off. Finish 25 lines on Level Nine in the B game, and you'll be treated to a Russian fiddler playing Tchaikovsky. Finish Level Nine on Height One in B and you get two Russians. By the time you reach Level Nine, Height Five, there are nine strumming and dancing Russians, followed by the slow, majestic launch of a space shuttle. The latter vignette is worth enduring all the pain it takes to get to it!

Strategy: Only general strategies apply, since every screen is changed by the placement of Tetrads. *Tetris* is largely a game of common sense—for instance, only a Flat Tetrad can complete a Tetris—but there are still a few strategies that may not be readily apparent:

• If you get one of the Z-shapes at the start, move it to one side or the other and slide another piece under its open end. If you get them later in the round, when Tetrads are piling up, *don't* place them so that there's an empty space beneath them unless you have absolutely no choice. Push them to any flat surface at least two squares long and wait for the next L-shape. Burying open spaces deep within the pile not only eats up room, it makes the job of constructing Tetrises more difficult—and dangerous, since there's less room to the top of the screen!

• Try, always, to leave a Block sticking up *somewhere* on a flat surface. That will save you the trouble of having to stand a Z-shape on end and then slide another piece under it.

• If a T-shape is descending, and a Z-shape is next, remember that the former is more versatile. Don't use a space that is the only one that would have accommodated a Z-shape!

• When a Flat Tetrad comes along, don't automatically plug it into the *lowest* spot in the pile just to complete a line or two. It's better to slip it where it will be most useful: in a spot which an upside-down L-shaped Tetrad is too short to fill.

• There's nothing wrong with dropping a T-shape Tetrad into a space large enough for an upside-down L-shape, provided the entire T-shape will disappear when the lines do. Otherwise, you'll trap a space below it. This holds true for any Tetrad you want to drop into a slot you designed for a larger piece—such as using a Z-shape on its side instead of a Flat Tetrad.

• If things are getting tight at the top of the screen, push Tetrads to the sides as much as possible. The higher the pile gets, the tougher it will be to do that . . . so leave the middle open.

• When you play Level Nine, Height Five, the name of the game is to note what piece is coming, see where you want to put it, rotate it if necessary, and *then* shove it into place. Don't try moving it above where it belongs and then rotating it: turning a Tetrad takes room, and there's more of that the higher you are on the screen. In any case, you'll want to keep the pile as low as possible, since the higher it gets, the faster the Tetrads fall. In this game, you *really* have to know where the next Tetrad is going before it hits the screen; one bad move and you're usually cooked. A bad move, incidentally, is placing a Flat Tetrad upright in the top half of the screen. Not only does its height cause Tetrads to fall faster, but you have the added problem of having to shift them around the top of the Flat Tetrad. Another bad move is leaving a one-Block-wide column—that is, a column for a Flat Tetrad—on the far left or right. If the center section builds up, you won't be able to get a Flat piece over; failing that, you'll be hard-pressed to finish a row. A *good* move on this level is to fill in the sides first, simply because they *are* the toughest to get to. Never mind Flat Tetrads: it's difficult rotating *any* pieces to get them into place on the sides once the middle begins to fill. When you start chewing the pile down and have five or six lines to go to win, don't worry so much about fitting Tetrads into the existing structure. Build up if you must, creating new lines to end the round. You'll hate yourself if you blow it with three or four lines to go!

• During the title screen, hold down on the pad, hit start, make your game selections, then start. When the game begins, you'll notice a heart symbol under the level indicator: this means you'll be playing the game super-quick!

Rating: A
Tetris is a time capsule–caliber classic, with levels of difficulty to please every player.

GAME BOY
MINI-TIPS

Before we go, here are a few quick tactics to use in other Game Boy games . . .

Deadheat Scramble
Execute level select as follows. On the title screen, press B eight times, A eight times, then B for as many levels as you want to go ahead. (Go to two by pressing one, for example.)

DuckTales
To defeat the Count at the end, you have to bop him on the bean. He's too high, you say? Reach him by leaping onto one of his Bats and vaulting from there to the vampire.

Golf
If you botch your Tee shot, shut off the machine as soon as you see where the ball's going, turn the game back on, and you'll be right back at the Tee!

Nemesis

Wait until the shooting starts, then hit pause. Move the pad up, up, down, down, left, right, left, right, hit the B button, A button, then Start. You'll resume the game with a host of power-ups.

To get a slew of options, Pause the game, then push up, up, down, down, left, right, left, and right. Push buttons B and A, then hit start: you'll have both Weapons, Shields, Missiles, and Lasers.

For Full Speed and Shield, use Pause, then push button B five times, A five times, and start the game again.

Penguin Wars

To choose your level in this game, pick a character on the character select screen, but *don't* leave the screen; simultaneously press left on the pad and B. Then press A and you'll bring up the level number. Hit up or down to change the numbers, then use Start to begin.

QBillion

Useful passwords are WALL, IDEA, and NOON.

Revenge of the Gator

If you can't get your pinball to enter the secret upper screen, use Pause to shut the flap and shut your ball inside.

Shanghai

A few interesting codes: MAN: tough level; REV: switches the Tiles so you can't see 'em until you've picked 'em; and STF gives you the credits.

Soccer Mania

To play invisible opponents, do this on the title screen: press up, up, down, down, left, right, left, right. Then hit B, A, then Start.

LYNX MINI-TIPS

. . . and here are passwords to get you through some of the top Lynx cartridges!

Chip's Challenge

Some passwords are: BDHP, JXMJ, ECBQ, YMCJ, TQKB, WNLP, FXQO, KCRE, VUWS, CNPE, DCKS, BTDY, COZQ, SKKK, AJMG, HMJL, KGFP, PQGV, YVYJ, IGGZ, UJDD, QGOL, BQZP, RYMS, PEFS, BQSN, NQFI, VDTM, NXIS, VQNK, BIFA, ICXY, YWFH, GKWZ, LMFU, UJDP, TXHL, OVPZ, HDQJ, LXPP, JYSF, PPXI, QBDH, IGGJ, PPHT, CGNX, ZMGC, SJES, FXJE, UBXU, YBLT, BLDM, ZYVI, RMOW, TIGW, GOHX, IJPQ, UPUN, ZIKZ, GGJA, RTDI, NLLY, GCCG, LAJM, EKFT, QCCR, MKNH, MJDV, NMRH, FHIC, GRMO, JINU, EVUG, SCWF, LLIO, OVPJ, UVEO, LEBX, FLHH, YJJS, WZYV, VCZO, OLLM, JPQG, DTMI, REKF, EWCS, BIFQ, WVHY, IOCS, TKWD, XUVU, QJXR. And a few special codes: JHEN, COZA, RGSK, DIGW, and MAND.

Electrocop
The passwords to doors in this game are:

Level	Password
One	2473, 9874, 8743
Two	3287, 5409
Three	9284, 7210, 3936, 7395, 8294
Four	0394
Five	8658, 5462, 9973, 7642, 0912, 0974, 7865, 4285
Six	8765
Seven	6021, 5824
Eight	7698
Nine	0170, 1092, 7102, 4726, 1375, 2857, 6998, 1798, 4391
Eleven	0293
Twelve	2987, 6443

Gates of Zendocon
The codes for each level are: BASE, ZYBX, XRXS, ANEX, NEAT, YARR, EYES, NYXX, ZYRB, SRYX, BARE, STAX, SZZZ, RAZZ, TRYX, STYX, YARB, BREX, SEBB, SNEX, ZAXX, BROT, STOB, XTNT, BOTZ, SNAX, TRAX, ZEBA, ROXY, NEXA, STAB, BOXX, TENT, NEAR, XRAY, RATT, NYET, NEXT, EBYX, ZEST, ZORT, BRAN, ROXX, NERB, TREY, STAR, SSSS, TERA, BYTE, BETA, ZETA.